How to Grow Your Leadership Skills

A Step-by-Step Guide to Cultivating Influence, Building Teams, and Inspiring Change

Ethan Empower

Copyright © Ethan Empower 2024

Ethan Empower

Acknowledgments:

We extend our sincere gratitude to everyone who contributed to the creation and realization of "How to Grow Your Leadership Skills: A Step-by-Step Guide to Cultivating Influence, Building Teams, and Inspiring Change." This book is a collaborative effort, and we are thankful for the support, insights, and dedication of all those involved.

Legal Notice:

This publication is provided with the understanding that the publisher and authors are not engaged in rendering legal, accounting, or other professional advice. The information contained within this book is for general informational purposes only and does not constitute the provision of legal advice. Readers are encouraged to seek professional advice pertaining to their specific situations.

While every effort has been made to ensure the accuracy and completeness of the information presented in this book, the publisher and authors assume no responsibility for errors or omissions or for damages resulting from the use of the information contained herein.

Disclaimer:

The views expressed in this book are those of the authors and do not necessarily reflect the official policy or position of any organization or entity mentioned within. Any resemblance to actual persons, living or dead, events, or locales is entirely coincidental.

The information presented in this book is based on the authors' experiences and research up to the time of publication. Given the dynamic nature of leadership and business environments, readers are advised to conduct additional research and seek updated information when making decisions.

The publisher and authors disclaim any responsibility for actions taken by readers based on the information provided in this book. The use of any product, service, or strategy mentioned in this book should be done with careful consideration and professional guidance.

Table of Contents

Introduction

The Power and Importance of Leadership

In today's fast-paced and ever-changing world, effective leadership has never been more critical. Whether it's in business, politics, community, or even our personal lives, strong leadership can be the difference between success and failure, progress and stagnation, inspiration and disillusionment.

Leadership, however, isn't about simply issuing orders or maintaining control. It's about empowering others, creating a vision, and leading by example. It's about making tough decisions, yet also being compassionate and understanding. It's about fostering teamwork and collaboration, but also promoting individual growth and autonomy.

Personal Journey in Leadership

My interest in leadership wasn't academic at first; it was born out of experience. I remember the first time I was placed in a leadership role. I was excited, of course, but also overwhelmed. I quickly realized that there was more to leadership than a title and a list of responsibilities.

Over the years, I've led teams of various sizes and dynamics, faced numerous challenges, and enjoyed many triumphs. I've learned from inspirational leaders and observed the consequences of poor leadership. These experiences, combined with extensive research and learning, have shaped my understanding of leadership, which I'm eager to share with you through this book.

Objectives and Structure of This Book

The aim of this book is to serve as a comprehensive guide to developing your leadership skills. Whether you're a new manager, an aspiring leader, or an experienced executive looking to refine your skills, this book will provide you with valuable insights and practical strategies.

In Part I, we'll explore the foundational elements of leadership, including self-awareness, emotional intelligence, decision making, and communication. In Part II, we'll delve into how to build and inspire your team by cultivating trust, leading by example, and empowering others. Part III will focus on the importance of continual learning and adaptability in leadership, and in Part IV, we'll guide you through creating your personal leadership development plan.

Each chapter will provide you with practical strategies, supported by real-life examples and exercises, to help you apply what you've learned in your own leadership journey.

I invite you to approach this book with an open mind and a willingness to reflect on your experiences, aspirations, strengths, and areas for improvement. As you delve into these pages, remember that leadership is not a destination, but a journey. And like any journey, it begins with a single step.

Welcome to your leadership journey.

Part I:

Understanding and Developing Core Leadership Skills

Chapter 1: Defining Leadership

Understanding leadership is a critical first step in our journey to enhance leadership skills. In this chapter, we will dive deep into the concept of leadership - its definition, the traits of effective leaders, and various leadership styles. By gaining a comprehensive understanding of leadership, you'll be better equipped to evaluate your own leadership approach and identify areas for development.

Leadership Vs. Management

One of the most common misconceptions about leadership is that it is synonymous with management. While there are overlaps between the two, they are fundamentally different concepts. In this section, we will dissect the differences between leadership and management, helping you understand the unique functions and responsibilities associated with each role.

Core Traits of Effective Leaders

What makes a leader effective? Are leaders born, or can leadership be learned? Through research findings and real-life examples, we'll explore the core traits commonly associated with effective leaders, such as emotional intelligence, integrity, vision, and the ability to inspire and motivate others.

The Different Styles of Leadership

Just as there is no one-size-fits-all approach to leading, there are various leadership styles, each with its strengths and weaknesses, and each effective in different situations. This section will introduce you to several key leadership styles, such as autocratic, democratic, transformational, and servant leadership. Understanding these styles will give you a wider range of tools to use in your leadership journey.

Effects of This Chapter

By the end of this chapter, you'll have a robust understanding of what leadership truly means, the traits of effective leaders, and the different leadership styles. This understanding is foundational to your growth as a leader. It's our starting point for reflecting on your leadership capabilities and how you can develop them further.

Remember, leadership is not just about a title or position. It's about influencing others towards achieving a common goal. As we journey through this chapter, I encourage you to keep an open mind, reflect on your own experiences, and consider how you can apply these insights to your unique leadership context.

Leadership Vs. Management

In understanding leadership, it's essential to differentiate it from management. Despite often being used interchangeably, they serve distinct roles within an organization, each vital in its own right. While both leadership and management contribute to organizational success, they involve different skills and focuses.

What is Management?

Management is the process of dealing with or controlling things or people. It involves planning, organizing, coordinating, and controlling resources—like personnel, finances, and operations—to achieve organizational goals. Managers ensure the smooth operation of the business on a day-to-day basis, focusing on processes, systems, and structures.

Managerial responsibilities often include:

1. **Planning and Budgeting:** Setting detailed steps and timetables to achieve the organization's goals, allocating necessary resources to ensure execution.

2. **Organizing and Staffing:** Assigning tasks, delegating responsibilities, establishing structures, recruiting personnel, and setting up rules and procedures.

3. **Controlling and Problem Solving:** Monitoring results, identifying deviations from the plan, and then planning and organizing solutions to these issues.

What is Leadership?

Leadership, on the other hand, goes beyond the administration and operational aspects of an organization. It involves inspiring, motivating, and influencing people to work towards a shared vision or goal. Leaders cultivate an environment that promotes growth, innovation, and collaboration.

Key roles of a leader include:

1. **Setting a Direction:** Developing a vision for the future and strategies for producing the changes needed to achieve that vision.

2. **Aligning People**: Communicating direction to those who can create coalitions that understand the vision and are committed to its achievement.

3. **Motivating and Inspiring:** Keeping people moving in the right direction by appealing to basic human needs, values, and emotions.

Why You Need Both Leadership and Management Skills

A well-balanced organization should have a mix of leaders and managers to succeed—each contributing unique value. Managers bring order and consistency by drawing up formal plans, designing rigid organizational structures, and monitoring results against the plans. Leaders, on the other hand, inspire and motivate their team, bring about change and innovation, and prepare for the future.

Effective leadership and management are not mutually exclusive. In fact, the most successful individuals are those who can both manage and lead. They can balance the need to achieve results with the necessity of inspiring their teams. They can implement and maintain processes while also driving change and innovation.

Importance of Leadership and Management Skills

Growing both your leadership and management skills is crucial for several reasons:

- **Increased Efficiency:** Good management skills ensure that tasks are completed efficiently and effectively, improving productivity and quality of work.

- **Employee Satisfaction:** Effective leadership fosters a positive work environment, which leads to higher employee satisfaction, lower turnover, and increased productivity.

- **Change Management:** In times of change or crisis, strong leadership is essential for motivating and guiding employees. At the same time, management skills are crucial for implementing these changes successfully.

- **Innovation:** Leadership encourages creativity and innovation, while management skills help turn these innovative ideas into reality.

- **Achieving Organizational Goals:** A combination of leadership and management ensures that the organization's vision is clear, and the steps needed to achieve that vision are effectively carried out.

In conclusion, while leadership and management are distinct concepts, they are both critical for personal and organizational success. The best leaders are also competent managers, and the best managers have strong leadership skills. As we continue our journey through this book, we will explore how you can develop and balance both these sets of skills to become a more effective leader and manager.

Core Traits of Effective Leaders

An effective leader is not defined merely by a specific set of skills, but also by their character and traits. These inherent and developed characteristics differentiate leaders from managers and contribute to their ability to inspire, motivate, and guide others. Let's delve into the core traits that define effective leaders.

❖ Integrity

Integrity is the foundation of leadership. It's about being honest, fair, and consistent in all actions and decisions. Leaders with integrity build trust, respect, and loyalty among their team members, fostering an environment where everyone feels valued and empowered.

❖ Emotional Intelligence

Emotional Intelligence (EI) refers to a leader's ability to recognize, understand, and manage their own emotions, as well as those of their team members. Leaders with high EI demonstrate empathy, effectively manage stress, make thoughtful and informed decisions, and successfully navigate social dynamics.

❖ Resilience

Leaders face various challenges and setbacks. Resilience—the ability to bounce back from adversity, learn from mistakes, and remain motivated in the face of difficulties—is key. Resilient leaders foster a culture of perseverance and tenacity within their teams.

❖ Vision

Great leaders have a clear, inspiring, and ambitious vision for the future. They can articulate this vision effectively to their team, inspiring them to strive towards the shared goal. Having a clear vision helps guide decision-making and strategy development.

❖ Influence

Effective leaders are able to influence others—not through coercion, but through inspiration, persuasion, and personal connection. They understand the needs, motivations, and emotions of their team members, and use this understanding to inspire action and commitment.

❖ Communication Skills

Leaders must be excellent communicators, able to convey ideas clearly and effectively. Good communication involves not only speaking but also listening and understanding others. Leaders who communicate effectively can motivate their teams, resolve conflicts, and ensure everyone is working towards the same goals.

Decisiveness

Leaders are often required to make tough decisions. Decisiveness—the ability to make firm decisions quickly and confidently—is critical. This trait, however, should be balanced with the ability to gather input from others, analyze situations carefully, and adjust decisions when necessary.

❖ Empathy

Empathy allows leaders to connect with their team members on a personal level, understanding their feelings, perspectives, and challenges. Empathetic leaders foster a supportive and inclusive work environment, leading to higher job satisfaction and improved team performance.

In sum, effective leadership is a blend of various traits. While some people may naturally possess some of these traits, most can be developed and refined over time. It's important to remember that no leader is perfect, and different situations may require different traits. The key is to remain open, self-aware, and committed to continual learning and growth.

As we proceed through this book, we will delve deeper into each of these traits, exploring how they impact leadership effectiveness and how they can be developed. The aim is not to transform you into a perfect leader, but to help you become a more effective one—aware of your strengths, conscious of your weaknesses, and committed to your personal leadership journey.

The Different Styles of Leadership

Effective leadership is not a one-size-fits-all proposition. Different situations and teams require different leadership approaches. Understanding various leadership styles can give you the flexibility to adapt your leadership approach depending on the situation, the task at hand, and the team you're leading. In this chapter, we'll explore several prominent leadership styles.

❖ Autocratic Leadership

Autocratic leaders tend to make decisions without consulting their teams. This style of leadership is typically most effective in situations where decisions need to be made quickly, or where the leader is the most knowledgeable member of the group. However, it can stifle creativity and can lead to low team morale if used excessively.

❖ Democratic Leadership

Democratic leaders, also known as participative leaders, encourage team members to participate in decision-making. They value open communication and input from their team, fostering an atmosphere of collaboration. This leadership style can lead to high job satisfaction and team commitment, but it may not be practical in situations that require quick decision-making.

❖ Transformational Leadership

Transformational leaders inspire and motivate their teams by setting a clear vision and leading by example. They prioritize the growth and development of their team members and encourage innovation. Transformational leaders can create a positive and inspiring work environment, but their success often depends on their ability to maintain team motivation.

❖ Transactional Leadership

Transactional leaders operate on rewards and punishments to motivate their teams. They set clear expectations and closely monitor their team's performance, rewarding good performance and reprimanding poor performance. This style can drive productivity and predictability but may limit creativity and initiative.

❖ Servant Leadership

Servant leaders prioritize the needs of their team above their own. They focus on personal growth, employee satisfaction, and team cohesion, believing that these elements will naturally lead to better organizational performance. Servant leadership can lead to high team morale and satisfaction, but it requires leaders who are comfortable with not being the center of attention.

❖ Laissez-faire Leadership

Laissez-faire leaders give their team members a high degree of autonomy, providing support and resources as needed but generally stepping back and letting the team work. This style can work well with highly skilled and motivated teams, but it can lead to poor performance if team members lack the skills or motivation to work independently.

❖ Situational Leadership

Situational leaders adapt their style based on the current situation, the capability and motivation of their team, and the task at hand. They are flexible, dynamic, and able to shift between leadership styles as required. This style can be highly effective but requires the leader to accurately judge situations and people's abilities.

Understanding these leadership styles is not about finding one "right" way to lead. Instead, it offers you a toolkit of styles that you can draw upon as situations dictate. As you grow and develop as a leader, you may find that you naturally gravitate toward one style, but the ability to adapt and draw on different styles when needed can greatly enhance your effectiveness as a leader.

The best leaders are versatile and adaptable, capable of adjusting their style to meet the needs of their team and the demands of the situation. Remember, leadership is a journey, and the more tools you have at your disposal, the more prepared you'll be to meet the challenges of this journey head-on.

Chapter 2: Self-Awareness and Emotional Intelligence

Chapter 2 delves into the realms of Self-Awareness and Emotional Intelligence, two indispensable facets of effective leadership. In this chapter, readers will embark on an introspective journey to understanding themselves better and learn how to harness their emotional intelligence to enhance their leadership capabilities.

Understanding Self-Awareness

The chapter begins with "Understanding Self-Awareness," elucidating what self-awareness means in the context of leadership. This section covers the benefits of being a self-aware leader, such as improved decision-making, increased empathy, and better interpersonal relationships. It emphasizes that a self-aware leader is well-positioned to understand their strengths, acknowledge their weaknesses, and implement personal development strategies.

Emotional Intelligence in Leadership

The next section, "Emotional Intelligence in Leadership," introduces the concept of Emotional Intelligence (EI) and its four key components: self-awareness, self-management, social awareness, and relationship management. The chapter highlights how EI underpins effective leadership by improving a leader's ability to manage their emotions, understand and empathize with others, handle stress, overcome challenges, and resolve conflicts.

Tools and Strategies to Enhance Self-Awareness and Emotional Intelligence

The final section, "Tools and Strategies to Enhance Self-Awareness and Emotional Intelligence," provides practical advice and techniques for developing these areas. It discusses approaches such as mindfulness meditation, journaling, seeking feedback, and emotional regulation exercises. The aim here is to equip readers with actionable strategies they can incorporate into their daily lives to boost their self-awareness and emotional intelligence.

Reading this chapter, readers will gain a solid understanding of the critical roles that self-awareness and emotional intelligence play in effective leadership. They will learn how to gauge their current levels of self-awareness and emotional intelligence and be provided with practical tools and strategies to enhance these. In turn, this will help them to become more empathetic and effective leaders, capable of fostering positive and productive relationships with their teams.

Understanding Self-Awareness

At the heart of leadership lies self-awareness. It's the foundational layer upon which all other leadership skills and competencies are built. Without a profound understanding of oneself, leading others becomes a difficult, if not impossible, task. In this chapter, we dive deep into the concept of self-awareness, its importance in leadership, and how to cultivate it.

In this chapter, readers will understand the importance of self-awareness in leadership and will gain practical strategies to enhance their self-awareness. By understanding themselves better, they will be better equipped to lead with authenticity, empathy, and effectiveness. This will not only help them in their personal development but will also foster a positive environment for their teams.

Definition of Self-Awareness

Self-awareness is the conscious understanding of one's own character, feelings, motives, and desires. It's the ability to take an honest look at yourself, to recognize and understand your thoughts, emotions, strengths, weaknesses, and behaviors, and understand how they affect both you and the people around you.

Why is Self-Awareness Important in Leadership?

Self-awareness is crucial in leadership for several reasons:

- **Decision Making:** Self-aware leaders are better equipped to make informed decisions because they understand their biases, preferences, and blind spots.

- **Emotional Regulation:** Being aware of your emotions allows you to manage them effectively, preventing them from clouding your judgment or leading to impulsive actions.

- **Empathy:** Understanding your emotions gives you an insight into how others might feel, fostering empathy—a critical leadership skill.

- **Self-Development:** Recognizing your strengths and weaknesses allows you to focus your personal development efforts effectively.

How to Cultivate Self-Awareness

Becoming more self-aware is a continuous journey of introspection and reflection. Here are some strategies to cultivate self-awareness:

- **Mindfulness Practice:** Mindfulness is about being present and fully engaged with whatever you're doing at the moment. Regular mindfulness practice, such as meditation, can help you become more aware of your thoughts, feelings, and reactions.

- **Journaling:** Writing down your thoughts, emotions, and reactions to different situations can give you insights into your patterns of thinking and behavior.

- **Feedback from Others:** Seeking constructive feedback from your peers, superiors, and subordinates can provide a fresh perspective and help you understand how others perceive you.

- **Psychological Assessments:** Tools such as the Myers-Briggs Type Indicator (MBTI) or the Emotional Quotient Inventory (EQi) can provide useful insights into your personality, preferences, and emotional intelligence.

Developing self-awareness is a lifelong journey, not a destination. As a leader, cultivating self-awareness can drastically improve your effectiveness and the quality of your relationships both in and outside the workplace. The benefits of self-awareness are far-reaching, and with practice, you'll continue to reap them throughout your leadership journey.

Emotional Intelligence in Leadership

Emotional intelligence (EI) is the ability to understand, use, and manage our emotions in a positive way to relieve stress, communicate effectively, empathize with others, overcome challenges, and defuse conflict. In leadership, emotional intelligence is a critical factor influencing a leader's ability to build relationships, influence others, and navigate social networks. In this chapter, we'll explore what emotional intelligence is, why it's crucial in leadership, and how you can develop it.

In this chapter, readers will have gained a thorough understanding of emotional intelligence and its vital role in leadership. They will be equipped with practical strategies to enhance their emotional intelligence, helping them to better manage their emotions and those of their teams, leading to more successful and effective leadership.

Understanding Emotional Intelligence

Coined by psychologists John Mayer and Peter Salovey, Emotional Intelligence is split into four key domains as popularized by psychologist Daniel Goleman:

- **Self-Awareness:** This is about recognizing and understanding our own emotions and how they affect our thoughts and behavior.

- **Self-Management:** This involves controlling impulsive feelings and behaviors, managing emotions in healthy ways, taking initiative, following through on commitments, and adapting to changing circumstances.

- **Social Awareness:** This is about understanding the emotions, needs, and concerns of others, picking up on emotional cues, and feeling comfortable socially.

- **Relationship Management:** This involves knowing how to develop and maintain good relationships, communicate clearly, inspire and influence others, work well in a team, and manage conflict.

Why Emotional Intelligence Matters in Leadership

Emotional intelligence plays a vital role in leadership for several reasons:

- **Improved Communication:** Leaders with high EI can convey their ideas more effectively, foster open communication within their teams, and build trust and respect.

- **Conflict Resolution:** EI gives leaders the skills to manage and resolve conflicts smoothly, ensuring that disagreements provide value to the decision-making process, rather than creating discord.

- **Better Teamwork:** Leaders high in EI can foster a more collaborative and inclusive team culture, ensuring every team member feels valued and heard.

- **Increased Empathy:** A leader with high EI can understand and share the feelings of others, a crucial trait for motivating employees, fostering loyalty, and promoting a positive work environment.

- **Resilience:** EI helps leaders maintain their composure and keep a positive outlook, even in the face of adversity and challenges.

Developing Your Emotional Intelligence

Cultivating EI involves strategies similar to those used for improving self-awareness, but also includes some additional steps:

- **Practice Empathy:** Try to see situations from others' perspectives. This can help you understand their reactions and build stronger, more meaningful relationships.

- **Improve Your Listening Skills:** Active listening involves fully focusing on the speaker, avoiding interruptions, and responding thoughtfully. This is a cornerstone of social awareness.

- **Manage Stress:** High stress levels can cloud your emotional clarity. Practice stress-reducing activities such as exercise, meditation, or simply taking a moment to pause and breathe during a hectic day.

- **Develop a Rich Emotional Vocabulary:** The better you can articulate your emotions, the better you'll understand them and be able to express them to others.

- **Seek Feedback:** Regularly ask others for their perspective on how you handle various situations. This can provide valuable insights into areas for improvement.

Emotional Intelligence is a critical component of effective leadership, influencing everything from decision-making to team dynamics. By investing in developing your EI, you can become a more effective, more approachable, and more resilient leader, paving the way for a more harmonious, productive work environment.

Tools and Strategies to Enhance Self-Awareness and Emotional Intelligence

Becoming a more self-aware and emotionally intelligent leader is not a one-time task, but a continuous journey. This chapter explores a variety of tools and strategies you can use to enhance your self-awareness and emotional intelligence, with practical steps you can take right away.

In this chapter, readers have gained a solid understanding of various tools and strategies to enhance self-awareness and emotional intelligence. By implementing these tools and strategies, they'll be able to lead more effectively and foster a positive, collaborative, and productive work environment.

Why Enhancing Self-Awareness and Emotional Intelligence is Essential

Improving self-awareness and emotional intelligence is critical for any leader who wishes to lead more effectively. A high level of self-awareness and emotional intelligence enables leaders to better understand their teams, make sound decisions, manage stress, resolve conflicts, and foster a positive work environment.

❖ Mindfulness and Meditation

Mindfulness and meditation are powerful tools for enhancing self-awareness and emotional intelligence. These practices help you become more aware of your thoughts and feelings, enabling you to manage them more effectively.

- **Mindfulness:** This involves focusing your attention on the present moment. You can practice mindfulness throughout your day, whether you're eating, walking, or engaged in a meeting.

- **Meditation:** This involves setting aside dedicated time to sit quietly and focus your mind, often on your breath or a mantra. Meditation can help reduce stress, improve concentration, and increase self-awareness.

❖ Reflective Journaling

Writing about your thoughts, feelings, and experiences can help you understand them more clearly. Regular journaling can help you identify patterns in your emotions and behaviors, leading to greater self-awareness. You can journal daily, weekly, or whenever you experience significant events or emotions.

❖ Feedback from Others

Getting feedback from colleagues, superiors, and subordinates can be an eye-opening experience. It gives you a different perspective on your behavior, skills, and performance, which you may have overlooked or not been aware of. Make sure to create an environment where people feel safe to share honest feedback.

❖ Emotional Intelligence Training

There are many workshops, seminars, online courses, and coaching programs available that focus on building emotional intelligence. These programs typically provide a combination of theory and practical exercises to help you understand and develop your emotional intelligence.

❖ Psychometric Tests

Psychometric tests such as the Myers-Briggs Type Indicator (MBTI), Emotional Quotient Inventory (EQi), or the DISC assessment can provide valuable insights into your personality traits, emotional intelligence, strengths, and areas for improvement.

These assessments often come with detailed reports and suggestions for development.

❖ Practicing Empathy

Empathy is a key aspect of emotional intelligence. To develop empathy, try to put yourself in other people's shoes. Listen attentively when others speak, validate their feelings, and respond with understanding.

Improving Self-Awareness:

- **Reflect on your emotions:** Regularly take time to consider your emotional state. Try to identify the emotions you're experiencing and why you're experiencing them.

- **Journaling:** Writing about your thoughts, emotions, and experiences can help you identify patterns and get a deeper understanding of your internal process.

- **Mindfulness practice:** Mindfulness helps you stay present and attentive to your current emotional state, allowing you to observe your feelings and thoughts without judgment.

- **Seek feedback:** Constructive feedback from colleagues, friends, and family can provide you with new perspectives and help you recognize any blind spots in your self-perception.

- **Psychometric tests:** Tools like the Myers-Briggs Type Indicator (MBTI) or the Emotional Quotient Inventory (EQi) can provide valuable insights into your personality traits and emotional tendencies.

Improving Emotional Intelligence:

- **Practice empathy:** Try to understand situations from others' perspectives. This will help you relate to their emotional responses and build stronger connections.

- **Respond instead of reacting:** Take a moment to process your emotions before responding in stressful situations. This can prevent emotional outbursts and regrettable decisions.

- **Manage stress:** Regular exercise, adequate sleep, and healthy eating habits can help maintain emotional balance. Mindfulness and relaxation techniques like yoga or deep breathing can also be beneficial.

- **Active listening:** Focus on understanding others' emotions and points of view during conversations. This can help improve your relationships and make others feel valued and understood.

- **Emotional regulation:** Recognize your emotional triggers and develop strategies to manage them effectively. This might include taking deep breaths, counting to ten, or momentarily stepping away from a situation to gather your thoughts.

- **Continual learning:** Attend workshops, read books, or take courses on emotional intelligence to deepen your understanding and learn new strategies for improvement.

Developing self-awareness and emotional intelligence is a continuous process. It requires time, effort, and dedication, but the rewards are worth it. As you become more self-aware and emotionally intelligent, you'll find that your relationships improve, your decision-making skills enhance, and your overall leadership effectiveness increases.

Chapter 3: Effective Decision Making

In the labyrinth of leadership, every turn represents a choice, and every choice can shape the destiny of an organization or team. Welcome to the intricate world of decision-making—a realm that intertwines logic, emotion, vision, and strategy. As leaders, the choices we make not only echo our values but also chart the course for our teams, our businesses, and ourselves.

In this chapter, we'll demystify the art and science of effective decision-making. Why is it that some leaders consistently make sound decisions, while others fall prey to biases and misjudgments? How can you ensure that your decisions, big or small, lead to the outcomes you desire? And when the stakes are high, how can you maintain clarity and purpose?

We'll embark on a comprehensive journey through the following sub-chapters:

The Role of Decision Making in Leadership:

Before we can refine our decision-making skills, we must first understand its integral role in leadership. This section will elucidate why good decision-making is paramount and how it can be the linchpin of influential leadership.

Common Traps in Decision Making:

Even the most seasoned leaders aren't immune to pitfalls. By recognizing common decision-making traps, you can navigate around them and ensure that your choices are rooted in clarity rather than obscured by bias.

Techniques for Better Decision Making:

Equipped with knowledge of potential pitfalls, we'll dive into actionable techniques that can significantly enhance your decision-making prowess. From tried-and-true methodologies to innovative approaches, this section offers a toolkit to empower every leader to make decisions with confidence.

Decision-making is a leadership skill that can be honed and refined. By understanding its nuances and intricacies, you'll be better positioned to lead with conviction, clarity, and purpose. Let's delve deep into the mechanisms of effective decision-making and unlock the secrets to mastering this vital leadership art.

The Role of Decision Making in Leadership

Decision making is a fundamental leadership competency, serving as the compass that directs a team or organization's journey. The role of a leader is often characterized by the decisions they make and, more crucially, the outcomes those decisions yield. In this chapter, we'll delve deep into the symbiotic relationship between leadership and decision making, understanding its significance, the timing, the 'how,' and the 'why' behind each resolution.

Why Decision Making is Central to Leadership

- **Direction and Vision:** At the core of leadership is the responsibility of setting a direction or vision for a team or organization.

This vision is carved out by a series of decisions, ranging from defining goals, allocating resources, to setting priorities.

- **Building Trust and Credibility:** Consistent, fair, and well-thought-out decisions build trust among team members. When employees believe their leaders make informed choices, they are more likely to trust and follow them.

- **Responsibility and Accountability:** Leaders are often held accountable for their choices. Effective decision making, therefore, safeguards the leader's credibility and, by extension, the organization's reputation.

When Leaders are Called to Decide

- **Daily Operations:** From resource allocation, personnel management, to setting daily priorities, leaders make decisions that influence day-to-day operations.

- **Crisis Situations:** In moments of crisis, swift and decisive action is required. Here, the quality of a leader's decision can mean the difference between escalation and resolution.

- **Strategic Planning:** Leaders make decisions about an organization's long-term direction and strategy, determining its trajectory for years to come.

- **Moral and Ethical Crossroads:** Often, leaders must decide on issues that aren't black and white but dwell in moral and ethical gray areas.

How Leaders Make Decisions

- **Information Gathering:** Effective leaders are informed leaders. They gather pertinent information, seek expert opinions, and consider relevant data before deciding.

- **Analytical Thinking:** Leaders often employ various analytical methods and tools to understand the potential outcomes of a decision.

- **Intuition:** Sometimes, decision-making requires leaders to rely on their gut feelings or intuition, especially when there's no precedent or data to lean on.

- **Collaborative Decision Making:** Leaders don't always decide alone. Collaborative decision making involves seeking input from team members or stakeholders.

- **Decisiveness:** After weighing all options, leaders must be decisive, standing firmly by their choices, and taking responsibility for the outcomes.

The Impact of Decision Making on Leadership Outcomes

- **Organizational Performance:** The cumulative effect of a leader's decisions can lead to organizational success or failure. From financial performance to team morale, decisions touch every facet of an organization.

- **Team Dynamics:** Decisions related to team composition, conflict resolution, and resource allocation can shape team dynamics, influencing collaboration, productivity, and morale.

- **Innovation and Growth:** Decision-making plays a pivotal role in innovation. Leaders decide on the allocation of resources to research and development, new projects, or exploring new markets.

The role of decision-making in leadership is profound and multifaceted. Every choice a leader makes casts ripples, influencing individuals, teams, and the broader organization. As we've explored, these decisions shape visions, build trust, and set strategic directions. They are the silent architects of organizational landscapes, carving out pathways of growth, innovation, and change.

The weight of decision-making, therefore, is a testament to its importance in leadership. For leaders who aspire to leave a positive, enduring mark on their organizations, mastering the art and science of decision-making is not just beneficial—it's imperative.

Common Traps in Decision Making

The path of decision-making is fraught with pitfalls. Even the most experienced leaders occasionally fall into traps that can skew their judgment and lead to suboptimal outcomes. Understanding these common traps is essential for any leader who wishes to navigate the labyrinth of decisions with clarity and confidence.

Why Leaders Fall into Decision-Making Traps

- **Cognitive Overload:** The human brain, while remarkable, has limits. In today's complex and fast-paced world, leaders often juggle multiple decisions simultaneously, leading to cognitive fatigue and vulnerability to errors.

- **Emotional Bias:** Leaders are humans first. Personal experiences, emotions, and deeply-held beliefs can cloud judgment and lead to biased decisions.

- **External Pressures:** Leaders often face pressures from stakeholders, shareholders, or the public, leading them to make decisions that may not align with the best interest of the organization.

Common Decision-Making Traps

- **Confirmation Bias:** This is the tendency to seek, interpret, and remember information that confirms one's pre-existing beliefs. Leaders might unknowingly give more weight to information that aligns with their current view and dismiss data that contradicts it.

- **Anchoring Bias:** Here, leaders give disproportionate weight to the first piece of information (the "anchor") they receive about a subject, influencing subsequent decision-making.

- **Overconfidence Bias:** Overestimating one's own knowledge or abilities can lead to rash decisions or inadequate risk assessment.

- **Availability Heuristic:** Leaders might make decisions based on recent information or experiences that are easily recalled, rather than comprehensive data.

- **Sunk Cost Fallacy:** Continuing a project or decision based on the amount already invested, rather than its current or future value.

- **Groupthink:** The desire for harmony or conformity in a group can lead to an irrational or dysfunctional decision-making outcome.

Where and When These Traps Manifest

- **High-Stress Environments:** In high-pressure situations, cognitive biases can become more pronounced, leading leaders to make rushed or poorly thought-out decisions.

- **Strategic Planning Sessions:** When charting out the long-term direction, leaders might rely on familiar strategies or ideas due to confirmation or anchoring biases.

- **Team Meetings:** The presence of strong personalities or the desire for consensus can lead to groupthink, stifling innovative or divergent ideas.

- **Resource Allocation:** When deciding where to invest resources, the sunk cost fallacy can prevent leaders from discontinuing projects that no longer provide value.

How to Avoid These Traps

- **Diverse Teams:** Encourage diversity of thought by building teams with varied experiences and backgrounds. Different perspectives can counteract biases and promote balanced decision-making.

- **Decision Frameworks:** Utilize structured decision-making frameworks to ensure a systematic approach, reducing the influence of biases.

- **Seek Feedback:** Encourage team members to speak up if they believe a decision is being influenced by a bias or external pressure.

- **Continuous Learning:** Regularly update yourself on cognitive biases and decision-making pitfalls. Being aware of them is the first step to avoiding them.

- **Reflective Practice:** Take time to reflect on past decisions, evaluate their outcomes, and identify any biases that may have influenced the process.

No leader is immune to the common traps of decision-making. However, by understanding and recognizing these pitfalls, leaders can arm themselves with the tools and strategies to navigate around them. The journey of leadership is a constant learning experience, and each decision, whether successful or not, provides a valuable lesson. By acknowledging and learning from these traps, leaders can continuously refine their decision-making prowess, ensuring they lead their organizations with clarity, wisdom, and vision.

Techniques for Better Decision Making

In the vast expanse of leadership, decision-making stands as both a challenge and an opportunity. Every decision reflects the leader's wisdom, intuition, and experience. While we've delved into the pitfalls that mar this process, it's now time to explore the techniques that can illuminate the path to better decisions.

Why Better Decision-Making Techniques Matter

- **Enhanced Outcomes:** Better decisions lead to better outcomes, positioning organizations for success and minimizing unintended consequences.

- **Reduced Regret:** A structured approach to decision-making can reduce the likelihood of future regrets, especially when tough choices are required.

- **Optimized Resource Allocation:** Effective decisions ensure that organizational resources—time, money, and manpower—are used efficiently and effectively.

- **Cultivating Trust:** Teams and stakeholders are more likely to trust leaders who make well-reasoned and consistent decisions.

Decision-Making Techniques: A Step-by-Step Guide

1. SWOT Analysis:

- **Definition:** A strategic planning tool used to evaluate Strengths, Weaknesses, Opportunities, and Threats.

- **How and When to Use:** Ideal for making strategic decisions, evaluating a project's viability, or assessing competitive position. Begin by listing down strengths and weaknesses (internal factors) and then opportunities and threats (external factors).

- **Why It's Beneficial:** It provides a comprehensive view of the current situation, helping leaders exploit strengths and opportunities while mitigating weaknesses and threats.

2. Decision Matrix:

- **Definition:** A table used to evaluate and prioritize a list of options and weigh them against specific criteria.

- **How and When to Use:** Useful when there are multiple options and criteria. Assign weights to each criterion, rate options against them, and then calculate a weighted score.

- **Why It's Beneficial:** Enables objective comparison of multiple options based on clear criteria, providing a visual guide to the best choice.

3. Cost-Benefit Analysis (CBA):

- **Definition:** A process used to weigh the total expected costs against the total expected benefits of a decision.

- **How and When to Use:** Applicable when financial implications are paramount. List all potential costs and benefits, then compare them to determine if benefits outweigh costs.

- **Why It's Beneficial:** Offers a clear financial perspective, ensuring that decisions make economic sense.

4. Brainstorming Sessions:

- **Definition:** A group creativity technique designed to generate a large number of ideas or solutions to a problem.

- **How and When to Use:** Best when a fresh perspective or creative solution is needed. Engage a diverse group, set a clear agenda, and encourage free thinking without immediate criticism.

- **Why It's Beneficial:** Harnesses collective intelligence, leading to innovative solutions and diverse perspectives.

5. The Delphi Technique:

- **Definition:** A structured communication technique, originally developed as a systematic forecasting method.

- **How and When to Use:** Employ when expert consensus is required. Engage experts to answer questions in multiple rounds, refining questions based on previous round responses until consensus is achieved.

- **Why It's Beneficial:** Reduces bias and leverages expert opinions, providing a well-rounded perspective.

6. Scenario Planning:

- **Definition:** A strategic planning method used to visualize possible future scenarios.

- **How and When to Use:** Ideal for long-term decisions with uncertain future implications. Develop multiple plausible future scenarios based on current trends and potential events.

- **Why It's Beneficial:** Prepares organizations for multiple eventualities, ensuring resilience and adaptability.

The journey to better decision-making is a continuous learning process. Each technique offers unique insights, catering to different scenarios and challenges. By equipping oneself with these methods and understanding when and how to employ them, leaders can confidently navigate the intricate paths of decision-making, consistently leading their organizations towards success and growth.

Chapter 4: Mastering Communication

In the theatre of leadership, communication is the script, the direction, and the performance. It's the magic that turns ideas into action, strategy into execution, and individuals into teams. While many consider communication to be a basic skill, mastering it is an art that sets exceptional leaders apart from the rest.

What This Chapter Offers

In Chapter 4, "Mastering Communication," we'll delve into the nuances that make communication an essential tool in your leadership arsenal. From the words you say to the body language you employ; every action sends a message. Here's what you can expect to learn:

- **Verbal, Non-Verbal, and Written Communication:** This section will dissect the three pillars of communication. While verbal skills often come to mind first, non-verbal cues and written formats also play a crucial role in how you are perceived as a leader.

- **Listening: The Underestimated Skill:** Most leaders are trained to speak; few are trained to listen. We will explore why listening is a vital component of effective communication and leadership, along with tips to improve your listening abilities.

- **Effective Communication Techniques:** Lastly, we'll provide you with a compendium of methods and best practices that will make your communications more engaging, more persuasive, and ultimately more effective.

Why You Should Read This Chapter

- **Elevate Your Leadership:** Good leaders know how to command a room; great leaders know how to engage everyone in it. Learn the fine art of communication to escalate your leadership from good to great.

- **Improve Team Dynamics:** Effective communication fosters better understanding and teamwork. Knowing how to get your message across clearly reduces misunderstandings and enhances productivity.

- **Enhance Personal Relationships:** Your role as a leader extends beyond the four walls of your office. Mastering communication skills can improve your personal relationships, making you more adept at managing conflicts and fostering stronger bonds.

- **Career Advancement:** Being a master communicator can open doors within your organization and in broader professional networks. From winning negotiations to inspiring teams, good communication is a ticket to career growth.

By the end of this chapter, you will not only understand the different facets of communication but also how to harness them effectively. Regardless of your current skill level, these insights will provide a comprehensive toolkit to make you a more proficient and effective communicator, both as a leader and as an individual.

Verbal, Non-Verbal and Written Communication

The ability to convey messages effectively is at the core of leadership. While the significance of communication is universally acknowledged, the complexity and diversity of it are often overlooked. This section aims to dissect three pillars of communication—Verbal, Non-Verbal, and Written—and explore their role, importance, and nuances in leadership.

Why Understanding Types of Communication is Essential

- **Enhanced Clarity:** Knowing which form of communication to use in different circumstances reduces ambiguity and fosters understanding.

- **Relationship Building:** Different communication types help establish rapport and trust, both within and outside the organization.

- **Conflict Resolution:** Effective communication is key to resolving misunderstandings and conflicts, allowing for smoother operation of the organization.

Verbal Communication

Verbal communication involves the use of words to share information with others. This can be face-to-face, over the phone, or via digital means like video conferences.

Importance in Leadership

- **Directness:** Allows for immediate feedback and clarification.
- **Nuance:** Tone, pitch, and volume can add layers of meaning or emphasis.

How, When, and Why to Use Verbal Communication

- **How:** Be clear, concise, and articulate. Make sure your tone matches the message.
- **When:** Use verbal communication for sensitive topics, urgent matters, or when immediate feedback is required.
- **Why:** It is fast, allows for back-and-forth discussion, and can be tailored on the fly to suit the dynamics of the conversation.

Non-Verbal Communication

Non-verbal communication involves transmitting messages without using words. This can include facial expressions, gestures, posture, and even tone of voice.

Importance in Leadership

- **Unspoken Cues:** These often reveal true feelings and attitudes, even when words might suggest otherwise.

- **Enhances Verbal Messages:** Gestures or facial expressions can provide emphasis or clarification to what is being verbally said.

How, When, and Why to Use Non-Verbal Communication

- **How:** Be aware of your body language and facial expressions. Make sure they align with your verbal messages.

- **When:** All the time. Non-verbal cues accompany verbal communication and can stand alone to convey meaning, especially in social and emotional contexts.

- **Why:** To provide a full spectrum of meaning and to add emphasis or subtlety to verbal messages.

Written Communication

Written communication involves any type of interaction that makes use of the written word, including emails, reports, and memos.

Importance in Leadership

- **Documentation:** Provides a record that can be referred to later.
- **Clarity and Detail:** Allows for comprehensive explanations, especially for complex ideas.

How, When, and Why to Use Written Communication

- **How:** Be precise and to the point. Use proper structure and grammar. Revise multiple times if needed.

- **When:** For formal communications, documentation, and when detailed instructions or explanations are required.

- **Why:** To provide a lasting record and to allow for complex ideas to be communicated clearly and at length.

Communication is multi-faceted, and each type has its unique advantages and disadvantages. Mastering the art of when and how to use verbal, non-verbal, and written communication can make a marked difference in your effectiveness as a leader. Understanding these modes is not just a leadership necessity but a foundational skill that will benefit you in every interaction, be it in the boardroom or at the dinner table.

Listening: The Underestimated Skill

While the ability to speak well is often spotlighted in leadership literature, the art of listening tends to go largely unrecognized. Yet, listening is not merely the act of hearing what someone is saying; it's an active process that involves attention, interpretation, and response. This part of the chapter aims to shine a light on this underappreciated skill, which is as integral to effective leadership as any other form of communication.

The Definition of Listening

Listening is the conscious process of hearing, interpreting, and responding to messages, whether they are verbal or non-verbal. It is a critical skill that transcends professional settings and enriches personal interactions.

Why Listening is Underestimated in Leadership

- **Spotlight on Speaking:** Public speaking and oratory skills often steal the limelight when discussing leadership qualities.

- **Misconception of Passivity:** Listening is often erroneously regarded as a passive skill, creating the illusion that it's easy or less important.

- **Lack of Formal Training:** Few leadership courses emphasize listening as a core skill, making it an often self-taught ability.

The Importance of Listening in Leadership

- **Decision Making:** Good listening skills can significantly enhance the quality of your decisions by enabling you to collect valuable input from team members.

- **Relationship Building:** Listening fosters trust and respect, allowing for more open and meaningful communication.

- **Emotional Intelligence:** Being a good listener boosts your emotional intelligence by improving your capacity for empathy and understanding.

Types of Listening

- **Active Listening:** This involves fully focusing, understanding, and then remembering and responding to what is being said.

- **Reflective Listening:** This includes reflecting the speaker's emotions and statements, often paraphrasing what has been said to demonstrate understanding.

- **Critical Listening:** Used particularly in meetings and discussions, this involves evaluating the logic and validity of what is being said.

Steps to Improve Listening Skills

Step 1: Prepare to Listen

Mentally Prepare: Clear your mind of distractions and focus on the speaker.

Step 2: Pay Full Attention

Non-Verbal Cues: Make eye contact, nod your head, and use other non-verbal cues to show engagement.

Step 3: Don't Interrupt

Let the Speaker Finish: Resist the urge to offer your thoughts until the speaker has completed their point.

Step 4: Reflect and Respond

Paraphrase: Summarize what you've heard in your own words to confirm your understanding.

Ask Questions: For further clarification, ask open-ended questions.

Step 5: Give Feedback

Express Appreciation: Thank the speaker for sharing their thoughts.

Listening is not just an underestimated skill; it's an underestimated art form that requires active engagement and a dedicated mind. By honing your listening skills, you not only amplify your leadership abilities but also enrich your personal life. Listening might be subtle, but its impact is anything but. It is a cornerstone for mutual respect, thoughtful decision-making, and overall effective leadership.

Effective Communication Techniques

As a leader, you're expected to be an excellent communicator. However, effective communication is more than just speaking well; it's an intricate blend of techniques that cater to different scenarios, audiences, and media. In this section, we'll delve into proven techniques that can elevate your communication skills, making you a more effective and impactful leader.

What is Effective Communication?

Effective communication is the ability to convey information, ideas, emotions, or thoughts clearly, concisely, and coherently, ensuring mutual understanding between the sender and the receiver. It encompasses various forms of communication:

verbal, non-verbal, and written, as well as the underrated skill of listening.

Why Effective Communication Techniques Are Important

- **Enhanced Teamwork:** Better communication leads to better collaboration.

- **Increased Productivity:** Clear instructions and feedback loops ensure that everyone knows what's expected.

- **Improved Relationships:** Good communication fosters trust and mutual respect.

Techniques for Effective Verbal Communication

Clarity and Conciseness

- How to Implement: Use simple words and direct sentences. Avoid jargon unless you're certain the audience understands it.
- Why it Works: This minimizes misunderstandings and makes the message more accessible.

Tone Matching

- How to Implement: Observe the emotional state of the audience and adjust your tone accordingly.
- Why it Works: It creates an emotional connection, making the audience more receptive to the message.

Techniques for Effective Non-Verbal Communication

Maintain Eye Contact

- How to Implement: Look people in the eye when speaking or listening to them.

Why it Works: It shows attentiveness and sincerity.

Controlled Body Language

- How to Implement: Keep your body language open and relaxed.
- Why it Works: It creates a welcoming environment and reinforces the message.

Techniques for Effective Written Communication

Structuring

- How to Implement: Always have a clear introduction, body, and conclusion.
- Why it Works: It helps the reader follow the argument or information.

Proper Grammar and Punctuation

- How to Implement: Proofread multiple times and consider using grammar-checking tools.
- Why it Works: Errors can distract from the message and affect your credibility.

Techniques for Effective Listening

Active Note-taking

- How to Implement: Jot down important points as you listen, but don't let it distract you from the ongoing conversation.

Why it Works: It aids in retaining and recalling information.

Paraphrasing and Summarizing

- How to Implement: Reflect back what you've heard by rephrasing it in your own words.

- Why it Works: It confirms understanding and gives the speaker a chance to clarify if needed.

Mastering Adaptability: The Ultimate Technique

Knowing how to adapt your communication style to different scenarios and people is the hallmark of a great leader.

- How to Implement: Be observant, be empathetic, and be willing to switch techniques as needed.
- Why it Works: No two situations or audiences are exactly the same. Adaptability ensures that your message will always hit the mark.

Effective communication isn't just a tool for leadership; it's the platform upon which all other leadership skills are built. Understanding and implementing these techniques will not only make you a more effective communicator but also a more effective leader. Whether you're conducting a meeting, sending an email, or having a one-on-one conversation, these techniques can help ensure that your message is conveyed as intended, thus enabling a more harmonious and productive work environment.

Part II: Building and Inspiring Your Team

Chapter 5: Building Trust and Credibility

In the realm of leadership, trust and credibility are not merely nice-to-have attributes; they are essential foundations upon which successful leadership is built. This chapter aims to shed light on the pivotal role that trust and credibility play in effective leadership. From highlighting their significance to providing actionable steps for building and sustaining them, this chapter serves as a comprehensive guide for leaders who aspire to be not just followed, but truly respected.

In this chapter, we will delve into the following sub-sections:

The Importance of Trust and Credibility in Leadership

In this segment, we will explore why trust and credibility are indispensable in leadership. These are the cornerstones that influence team cohesion, job satisfaction, and ultimately, organizational performance.

Actions That Build Trust and Credibility

Trust and credibility don't magically appear; they are built over time through consistent actions. This section will offer a roadmap of specific actions you can take to earn the trust and credibility you need to be an effective leader.

Overcoming Setbacks in Trust and Credibility

No leader is perfect; setbacks are inevitable. What sets a great leader apart is the ability to rebuild trust and restore credibility. This section will provide strategies and insights on how to bounce back effectively.

By the end of this chapter, you should have a well-rounded understanding of why trust and credibility are paramount, how to build them through consistent and authentic actions, and how to recover when you've hit a bump in the road. Armed with this knowledge, you'll be better equipped to foster a culture that not only respects your leadership but is also motivated to strive for collective success.

The Importance of Trust and Credibility in Leadership

Trust and credibility are often mentioned in leadership discourses but are seldom dissected to reveal their intricate details and enormous influence. This section aims to fill that gap by diving deep into why these qualities are non-negotiables in effective leadership. We'll also explore how they're interrelated and how their presence or absence can profoundly impact an organization.

What are Trust and Credibility?

- **Trust:** Trust is the belief or confidence that one party has in the reliability, integrity, and honesty of another party. In a leadership context, trust is a multi-dimensional construct involving not just the leader's trust in their team, but also the team's trust in the leader.

- **Credibility:** Credibility refers to the quality of being trusted and believed in. It is an assessment of the leader's competence and character, judged not only by what they say but also by what they do.

Why Trust and Credibility Matter in Leadership

Boosts Team Morale

- Why: When team members trust their leader, they are more likely to be engaged and committed.
- How: Leaders can boost morale by consistently being honest and transparent in their dealings.

Enhances Collaboration

- Why: Trust facilitates an open exchange of ideas, leading to more effective collaboration.

- How: Creating a culture where everyone feels their voice is valued.

Increases Productivity

- Why: Employees are more motivated and work more efficiently when they find their leaders credible.

- How: Setting clear expectations and giving timely, constructive feedback.

The Interplay Between Trust and Credibility

Trust and credibility are deeply interwoven. Credibility forms the basis upon which trust is built. A credible leader is more likely to be trusted, and a trusted leader is generally considered credible.

Why: Each quality reinforces the other, creating a virtuous cycle.

- How: Consistency in actions and words is key. For example, if a leader commits to an open-door policy and follows through, they gain both trust and credibility.
- The Domino Effect: How Lack of Trust and Credibility Can Derail Leadership

Decreased Employee Retention

- Why: Talented employees are less likely to stay in an environment where they don't trust the leadership.
- How: A lack of trust creates a toxic work environment, impacting overall job satisfaction.

Reduced Innovation

- Why: People are less likely to take risks or think outside the box if they don't trust their leader's judgment or credibility.

- How: Employees may hesitate to share new ideas for fear of retribution or dismissiveness.

Building Blocks of Trust and Credibility

- Transparency: Clear, open communication about decisions, and changes.
- Consistency: Align actions with words.
- Accountability: Taking responsibility for one's actions, including mistakes.

Trust and credibility are not mere buzzwords but the very bedrock of effective leadership. They have a cascading effect on every aspect of an organization, from individual performance to overall business metrics. Understanding their importance and the steps to build them is imperative for anyone aspiring to lead successfully.

The subsequent sections of this chapter will delve deeper into the actionable steps for building and sustaining trust and credibility, as well as strategies for recovery after setbacks. By investing in these essential qualities, you invest in the long-term health and success of your organization.

Actions That Build Trust and Credibility

After understanding the significant role that trust and credibility play in effective leadership, it's crucial to delve into the actions that can help build these attributes. This part of the chapter is designed to be a practical guide, focusing on actionable steps that can lead to a robust foundation of trust and credibility in any leadership role.

Key Actions that Build Trust

1. Open and Honest Communication

- Why: Transparency builds trust. Team members feel valued and respected when they are kept in the loop.

- How: Regular team meetings, open-door policies, and honest discussions about challenges and opportunities.
- When: Consistency is key; make it a routine part of your leadership style.

2. Demonstrating Reliability

- Why: Being reliable creates a stable and predictable environment, which is fundamental for trust.
- How: Follow through on promises and commitments. If you say you'll do something, make sure it gets done.
- When: Always, without exception.

Key Actions that Build Credibility

1. Expertise and Competence

- Why: A leader must be competent in their field to be considered credible.

- How: Continual learning and professional development. Don't just rest on past achievements.
- When: Ongoing. The business landscape changes, and so should your skillset.

2. Integrity

- Why: Actions speak louder than words. Integrity is about aligning your actions with your words and values.
- How: Be honest, even when it's difficult. Take responsibility for both successes and failures.
- When: Every moment of every day. Integrity isn't a part-time job.

Actions That Serve Both Trust and Credibility

1. Accountability

- Why: Being accountable for one's actions fosters both trust and credibility.

- How: Own up to mistakes, learn from them, and take steps to correct them.

- When: Immediately upon realizing an error or oversight has occurred.

2. Consistency

- Why: People trust and believe in leaders who are consistent in their actions and decisions.

- How: Develop consistent habits and routines that reflect your commitments and values.

- When: Consistency should be a constant effort.

3. Empathy and Understanding

- Why: Showing understanding and empathy for team members' challenges builds trust and signals emotional intelligence, which enhances credibility.

- How: Listen actively and respond with empathy to team members' concerns and feedback.
- When: Whenever you interact with team members, but especially during difficult or challenging times.

The Cumulative Effect of These Actions

These actions are not standalone measures but are interrelated steps in building a strong foundation of trust and credibility.

- Why: Each action feeds into and amplifies the other, creating a virtuous cycle of trust and credibility.
- How: Consistent and repeated practice of these actions over time.
- When: From day one of your leadership tenure and every day after.

Pitfalls to Avoid

- Mixed Signals: Inconsistency between your words and actions can rapidly erode both trust and credibility.
- Lack of Transparency: Hiding information or not being upfront can cause skepticism and mistrust.

Building trust and credibility is not an overnight process; it's a continuous endeavor that demands consistent effort, vigilance, and sincerity. By consciously incorporating these actions into your leadership style, you'll not only build trust and credibility but also create a positive, productive work environment.

In the next section, we will discuss strategies for overcoming setbacks in trust and credibility, because even the best leaders can make mistakes. The mark of a great leader, however, is how effectively they bounce back from those setbacks.

Overcoming Setbacks in Trust and Credibility

Leadership is not a perfect art. Mistakes and setbacks are inevitable. What distinguishes excellent leaders is not the absence of errors but their ability to recover from them and rebuild the trust and credibility that may have been lost. This section explores how to handle setbacks in trust and credibility effectively.

The Importance of Addressing Setbacks

- Why: Ignoring issues can make them worse, causing further erosion of trust and credibility.

- How: Act promptly to acknowledge the problem. Sweeping issues under the rug can exacerbate mistrust.

- When: As soon as you're aware of the setback. Timeliness is crucial.

Common Reasons for Setbacks in Trust and Credibility

1. Broken Promises

- Why: Failing to keep a commitment can seriously undermine both trust and credibility.
- How: Make realistic commitments and be transparent if you foresee a failure.

2. Inconsistent Behavior

- Why: Inconsistency confuses people and erodes trust.
- How: Always align your actions with your words and commitments.

3. Lack of Transparency or Dishonesty

- Why: Any form of dishonesty is a trust killer.
- How: Always be transparent and honest, even when the truth is uncomfortable.

Steps to Rebuild Trust and Credibility

Step 1: Acknowledge the Mistake

- Why: Ignoring or downplaying mistakes can make the situation worse.
- How: Admit the mistake openly and accept responsibility.
- When: As soon as you're aware of it.

Step 2: Understand the Impact

- Why: Understanding the extent and nature of the impact helps in crafting a suitable response.
- How: Communicate with stakeholders to gauge the impact.

Step 3: Make Amends

- Why: Actions speak louder than words.
- How: Take concrete steps to rectify the situation and prevent future occurrences.

Step 4: Re-establishing Consistency

- Why: Consistency rebuilds trust over time.
- How: Align your future actions to commitments and maintain this alignment.

Navigating the Emotional Terrain

- Why: Emotional reactions can complicate the path to rebuilding trust.
- How: Use emotional intelligence to manage the situation. Be empathetic and responsive but not reactive.

Long-term Strategies

Establish a Culture of Openness

- Why: An open culture fosters trust.

- How: Encourage feedback and transparent communication.

Continuous Monitoring

- Why: Trust and credibility need to be maintained.
- How: Regularly assess the state of trust and credibility in your team.

Setbacks in trust and credibility are challenging but surmountable obstacles in leadership. With prompt action, emotional intelligence, and a genuine commitment to change, leaders can regain lost trust and restore their credibility. The next section will delve into another vital leadership attribute: the ability to inspire and motivate a team.

Rebuilding trust and credibility isn't just about managing a crisis; it's about laying down a consistent pattern of trustworthy behavior over

time. It's a long-term investment in your leadership
journey.

Chapter 6: Leading by Example

Leadership is not just about directing others; it's about inspiring them through your own actions. In this pivotal chapter, we dive deep into the concept of "Leading by Example," a critical skill set that goes beyond mere words and moves into the territory of actions and behaviors. By the end of this chapter, you will gain valuable insights into why, how, and when to use your own behavior as a model for your team's conduct.

1. The Power of Role Modeling

In this section, we will discuss the impact that a leader can have by acting as a role model. You'll discover how your actions can have a far-reaching influence on your team's behavior, attitudes, and even their long-term growth. We'll delve into why role modeling is more effective than directive leadership styles and offer practical tips on how you can be a better role model.

2. Maintaining Consistency with Your Values and Principles

Leadership can sometimes feel like a balancing act, especially when it comes to maintaining consistency in your actions. Here, we'll explore the necessity of aligning your behavior with your stated values and principles. This isn't just about 'walking the talk'; it's about demonstrating integrity and earning respect. You'll learn strategies for ensuring that your actions consistently reflect your core beliefs, even when faced with challenging decisions.

3. Leading Through Challenges and Change

Leadership is often tested during times of organizational upheaval or significant challenges. This section is designed to equip you with the skills to maintain your role as an exemplary leader during difficult times. You'll learn why your actions during these challenging periods are particularly impactful and get hands-on advice for navigating complexities while keeping your team inspired and focused.

In essence, this chapter aims to provide you with a comprehensive guide to leading by example. Whether you're a seasoned leader or stepping into a leadership role for the first time, the principles and strategies laid out in this chapter will offer actionable insights to enhance your leadership skills effectively. We will explore these topics through real-life examples, case studies, and actionable steps so you can immediately apply what you've learned.

The Power of Role Modeling

In leadership, one of the most powerful tools at your disposal is your ability to lead by example. Role modeling is not just about imitating behaviors; it's about embodying the qualities, attitudes, and actions that you wish to instill in your team. This part of the chapter delves into the intricacies of role modeling, its impacts, and how to maximize its effectiveness.

The Essence of Role Modeling

Role modeling is the act of exemplifying desirable behaviors, attitudes, and values that others, particularly subordinates, are encouraged to emulate. It's about demonstrating through your own actions the kind of conduct that is expected in a given environment.

Why it Matters

- **Influence:** As a leader, your actions carry significant weight and can influence your team's behavior more than your words.

- **Trust:** When you consistently exhibit the values and principles that you preach, it builds trust and credibility.

- **Cultural Influence:** Role modeling helps in shaping the culture of the organization by setting a standard for expected behaviors.

The Components of Role Modeling

1. Behavior

Your behavior encompasses your actions, reactions, and overall conduct. It's crucial that your behavior aligns with the values and expectations of your organization.

How to Model Behavior:

- **Consistency:** Ensure that your actions consistently reflect the values and principles you espouse.

- **Responsibility:** Accept responsibility for your actions and the consequences that follow.

2. Attitude

Your attitude reflects your disposition, mindset, and approach to situations.

How to Model Attitude:

- **Positivity:** Maintain a positive attitude, even in challenging situations.

- **Resilience:** Demonstrate resilience by bouncing back from setbacks and maintaining a constructive outlook.

3. Values

Values are the principles that guide your decisions and actions.

How to Model Values:

- **Integrity:** Act with honesty and integrity in all situations.

- **Empathy:** Show empathy and understanding towards others' perspectives and feelings.

The Impact of Effective Role Modeling

1. Enhances Learning

Role modeling facilitates learning by providing a tangible example for others to follow. It's easier for people to understand and adopt behaviors when they see them in action.

2. Builds a Stronger Team Culture

Consistent role modeling helps in establishing a strong and cohesive team culture. It sets the tone for what is acceptable and expected within the team.

3. Facilitates Change

Role modeling is a powerful tool for facilitating change. When leaders embody the changes they wish to see, it encourages others to follow suit.

Common Pitfalls in Role Modeling

1. Inconsistency

Inconsistency between your words and actions can undermine your credibility and confuse your team.

2. Lack of Self-Awareness

Being unaware of your own behavior and its impact on others can lead to unintended consequences.

3. Overemphasis on Perfection

Striving for perfection can create an unrealistic standard for your team and may discourage them from trying.

Strategies for Effective Role Modeling

1. Be Aware of Your Actions

Regularly reflect on your actions and consider how they may be perceived by others.

2. Seek Feedback

Actively seek feedback from your team and other stakeholders to understand the impact of your actions.

3. Practice What You Preach

Ensure that your actions align with your words and the values you espouse.

4. Be Authentic

Authenticity is key to effective role modeling. Be genuine in your actions and interactions.

Role modeling is a powerful tool in a leader's arsenal. By embodying the values, attitudes, and behaviors you wish to instill in your team, you can influence their conduct, build a stronger team culture, and facilitate change. However, it's essential to be aware of your actions, seek feedback, and strive for authenticity to maximize your impact as a role model.

In the next section, we will explore how to maintain consistency with your values and principles, which is a crucial aspect of leading by example.

Maintaining Consistency with Your Values and Principles

One of the core challenges leaders face is maintaining consistency between what they say and what they do. It's one thing to articulate great values; it's another thing entirely to consistently act upon them. This section delves into how you can maintain this consistency, a critical aspect that lends credibility to your leadership and provides a strong model for your team to follow.

The Importance of Consistency

Consistency, in the context of leadership, refers to the alignment of actions, decisions, and behaviors with stated values and principles over a period of time.

Why Consistency Matters

- **Credibility:** Consistency builds your credibility as a leader. People are more likely to trust you if your actions match your words.

- **Predictability:** It provides a predictable environment, making it easier for team members to understand what is expected of them.

- **Integrity:** Consistency is a demonstration of integrity, cementing the idea that you are dependable and reliable.

Understanding Values and Principles

Values

These are the core beliefs that guide your behavior and decisions. Examples might include honesty, respect, and integrity.

Principles

Principles are the rules and guidelines set based on your values. They define how you interact with others and approach your work.

How to Define Your Values and Principles:

- **Self-Reflection:** Take time to introspect and identify what matters most to you.

- **Consultation:** Seek input from trusted colleagues, mentors, and even team members.

- **Documentation:** Write down your values and principles to make them concrete.

Strategies for Maintaining Consistency

1. Self-Awareness

Being aware of your actions and their implications is the first step towards consistency.

Daily Reflection: End each day by evaluating if your actions aligned with your values.

2. Feedback Loops

Create systems for regular feedback from your team and other stakeholders.

Anonymous Surveys: These can provide honest insights into whether your team believes you are acting consistently.

3. Alignment with Team and Organizational Goals

Your values and principles should not only align with your personal beliefs but also with your team's and organization's goals.

Regular Check-ins: Consistently revisit team and organizational goals to ensure they align with your actions.

4. Navigating Conflicts

Sometimes values can conflict with each other or with immediate goals.

Prioritization: Learn to prioritize values in conflicting situations and communicate your reasoning to your team.

Common Challenges in Maintaining Consistency

1. Changing Circumstances

Dynamic work environments may force you to adapt, but that adaptation should not come at the cost of your core values.

2. Pressure to Conform

There may be pressure to align with prevailing attitudes or practices that conflict with your values.

3. Complexity in Implementation

Sometimes, maintaining consistency in every decision and action can become complex and exhausting.

Leaders Who Lost Credibility: We'll explore real-life examples where a lack of consistency led to a loss of credibility and the consequences that followed.

Success Stories: An in-depth look at leaders who have successfully maintained consistency, providing actionable insights and inspiration.

Consistency in aligning your actions with your values and principles is a cornerstone of effective leadership. It requires a concerted effort, from self-awareness to soliciting feedback and ensuring alignment with both personal and organizational goals. Navigating this complex landscape is challenging but essential for leaders aiming to lead with authenticity and integrity.

In the following section, we will delve into the complexities of leading through challenges and change, another key area where your ability to maintain consistency will be put to the test.

Leading Through Challenges and Change

The ultimate test of a leader is not how you perform during times of comfort and convenience but how you handle challenges and change. Leaders are often judged based on their ability to steer their teams through difficult times. In this chapter, we will explore the intricacies of leading in the face of challenges and the dynamics of managing change effectively.

The Importance of Leading Through Challenges

Leading through challenges refers to the practice of guiding and inspiring a team when faced with difficulties or obstacles that could potentially hamper objectives or well-being.

Why It Matters

- **Resilience:** A team's ability to bounce back from challenges often depends on strong leadership.

- **Morale:** A leader's approach to challenges has a significant impact on team morale.

- **Trust:** Successfully navigating through difficulties builds trust within the team.

- **Legacy:** How a leader handles challenges often defines their legacy.

Identifying Types of Challenges

External Challenges

- Market Competition
- Economic Downturn
- Regulatory Changes

Internal Challenges

- High Employee Turnover
- Poor Team Dynamics
- Lagging Productivity

Personal Challenges

- Work-Life Balance
- Stress Management
- Ethical Dilemmas

Techniques for Leading Through Challenges

1. Assess the Situation

- Data Gathering: Collect information to understand the scope and impact of the challenge.
- Consult Team Members: Get input from various stakeholders for a fuller perspective.

2. Formulate a Plan

- SWOT Analysis: Identify Strengths, Weaknesses, Opportunities, and Threats related to the challenge.
- Action Plan: Develop a step-by-step plan with milestones.

3. Communicate Effectively

- Transparency: Be honest about the challenges while also instilling a sense of hope.
- Feedback Loop: Keep lines of communication open for updates and feedback.

4. Execute and Adapt

- Implementation: Carry out the action plan while continuously monitoring its effectiveness.
- Adjustments: Be willing to adapt the plan as you go along, based on results and feedback.

The Dynamics of Change Management

Change management is the process of helping individuals and organizations transition from a current state to a desired future state.

Steps in Change Management

- **Preparation:** Understand the change that is needed and prepare the team.

- **Implementation:** Roll out the change while managing resistance and encouraging adoption.
- **Review:** Assess the impact of the change to ensure it meets its objectives.

Balancing Continuity and Change

- **Consistency:** Maintain your leadership style and principles, even as you adapt to new circumstances.

- **Flexibility:** Be willing to take innovative approaches when faced with unprecedented challenges.

Leaders in Crisis: Analyzing the leadership styles of those who have effectively managed crises.

Change Management Failures: Learning from situations where change was not effectively managed.

Leading through challenges and change is a complex, but essential, part of leadership. The ability to guide a team through difficulty while also effectively managing change can be the difference between organizational success and failure. Employing thoughtful techniques and strategies for dealing with these challenges can help ensure that you not only survive these trials but also come out stronger.

The next section will delve into another aspect of leadership that complements everything we've discussed so far: building relationships with team members and stakeholders to form a cohesive and effective unit.

Chapter 7: Empowering and Motivating Others

In the heart of our narrative lies Chapter 7, a pivotal exploration into the multifaceted nature of leadership—beyond the realm of authority, into the realms of empowerment and motivation. Here, the characters embark on a transformative journey, realizing that true leadership lies not just in personal achievement but in the ability to uplift and inspire those around them.

1. The Leader as a Coach:

In the opening sub-chapter, "The Leader as a Coach," readers witness a profound shift in our protagonists' approach to leadership. No longer confined to making decisions from a position of authority, our characters embrace the role of mentors. Through coaching, they discover the power of investing in their team members' growth. As the characters guide, nurture, and unlock the latent potential within their colleagues, they come to understand that leadership is a collaborative journey of continuous development.

Key Insights:

- *Leadership evolves into a dynamic exchange of knowledge and growth.*
- *The transformative impact of mentorship on individual and collective success.*

2. Techniques to Motivate and Empower:

The narrative then unfolds into the second sub-chapter, "Techniques to Motivate and Empower." Here, the characters wield a diverse set of leadership tools to cultivate motivation and empowerment within their team. From recognizing and leveraging individual strengths to creating an environment that fosters innovation, our protagonists navigate the nuances of effective leadership. Through real-world examples and challenges, readers gain practical insights into how motivation becomes the catalyst for achieving shared goals.

Key Insights:

- *Recognition of individual strengths as a cornerstone of motivation.*
- *Creating a positive work culture that fuels innovation and collaboration.*

3. Constructive Feedback and Performance Management:

The journey reaches its zenith with the third sub-chapter, "Constructive Feedback and Performance Management." Our characters grapple with the delicate art of providing constructive feedback—a crucial element in shaping individual and collective performance. As they navigate through performance evaluations and feedback sessions, readers witness the characters striking a balance between accountability and support. This section underscores the importance of feedback as a powerful tool for continuous improvement.

Key Insights:

- *Constructive criticism as a catalyst for personal and professional development.*
- *The nuanced approach to performance management within a supportive framework.*

Key Takeaways:

- *Leadership transcends individual success to encompass the empowerment and motivation of others.*
- *The leader as a coach plays a pivotal role in fostering continuous growth and development.*

- *Techniques for motivation include the strategic recognition of individual strengths and the creation of a positive work culture.*
- *Constructive feedback is a powerful tool for performance management and overall improvement.*

As our characters venture deeper into the realms of empowerment and motivation, readers are invited to witness the intricate dance of leadership, where success is measured not only by personal achievements but by the collective growth and inspiration that ripple through the entire team. This chapter serves as both a guide for aspiring leaders and a narrative tapestry that leaves readers eagerly anticipating the transformative leadership moments that lie ahead.

The Leader as a Coach

In the ever-evolving landscape of leadership, the role of a leader has transcended mere command and control. A paradigm shift is witnessed in the form of a leader embracing the role of a coach, recognizing the immense potential for growth and success that lies within each team member. This chapter unravels the layers of "The Leader as a Coach," exploring the profound impact coaching has on fostering individual and collective excellence.

Why Coaching Matters:

Coaching, in the context of leadership, refers to a collaborative and developmental approach where a leader assumes the role of a mentor, guiding and supporting team members to maximize their potential and achieve their professional and personal goals.

The essence of coaching lies in the belief that every individual possesses unique strengths and talents waiting to be unearthed. A coach-leader understands that by unlocking these potentials, the entire team benefits, leading to heightened performance, job satisfaction, and a culture of continuous improvement.

How to Coach Effectively:

1. Establish Trust and Rapport:

The foundation of effective coaching is built on trust. Leaders must cultivate an open and trusting environment where team members feel comfortable sharing their aspirations, challenges, and concerns.

2. Active Listening:

Coaching necessitates attentive and active listening. Leaders must listen not only to words but also to the emotions and nuances behind them. This enables a deeper understanding of team members' perspectives.

3. Goal Setting:

Collaboratively set clear, achievable, and measurable goals. These goals should align with both individual aspirations and organizational objectives. Establish a roadmap for success with milestones and timelines.

4. Provide Constructive Feedback:

Constructive feedback is a cornerstone of coaching. Leaders must offer feedback in a supportive manner, highlighting strengths, addressing areas for improvement, and fostering a growth mindset.

5. Encourage Self-Reflection:

Coaching involves guiding individuals toward self-discovery. Encourage team members to reflect on their own performance, identify areas for growth, and develop action plans for improvement.

6. Empower Through Questions:

Rather than providing all the answers, coach-leaders empower their team by asking thought-provoking questions. This stimulates critical thinking and encourages individuals to find solutions on their own.

When Coaching Is Most Effective:

1. During Transition Periods:

Coaching is particularly impactful during periods of change or transition. Whether it's a new project, role, or organizational shift, coaching helps individuals navigate uncertainties and adapt more effectively.

2. Skill Development:

When team members are acquiring new skills or working on personal development, coaching becomes a powerful tool for honing these abilities. It provides guidance, support, and a structured approach to skill enhancement.

3. Performance Improvement:

Coaching is instrumental when addressing performance challenges. Rather than punitive measures, a coaching approach helps individuals understand their performance gaps and collaboratively develop strategies for improvement.

4. Career Development:

For individuals aspiring to advance in their careers, coaching offers personalized guidance. Leaders can assist in creating development plans, identifying growth opportunities, and navigating career paths.

Key Takeaways:

- *Coaching is a Collaborative Journey:*

The leader as a coach engages in a collaborative journey with team members, fostering a sense of shared responsibility for success.

- *Individual Growth Catalyzes Collective Success:*

By focusing on the individual growth and development of team members, leaders enhance the collective capabilities of the entire team.

- *Trust is the Bedrock:*

Trust is the bedrock of effective coaching. Establishing a foundation of trust enables open communication and a conducive environment for growth.

- *Coaching is Adaptive:*

Effective coaching adapts to various situations, whether it's during times of change, skill development, performance improvement, or career advancement.

In the ongoing narrative of leadership, the leader as a coach emerges as a guiding force, nurturing the potential within each team member. As this coaching journey unfolds, leaders become architects of success, sculpting a workplace culture where continuous learning, development, and achievement are the norm. The ripple effects of effective coaching extend far beyond individual accomplishments, shaping the very fabric of organizational excellence.

Techniques to Motivate and Empower

In the dynamic landscape of leadership, the ability to motivate and empower team members is the cornerstone of building a resilient and high-performing organization. This chapter delves into the intricacies of "Techniques to Motivate and Empower," exploring the multifaceted strategies that leaders employ to inspire individuals and cultivate a culture of empowerment.

Why Motivation and Empowerment Matter:

Motivation is the internal or external force that prompts individuals to take action, achieve goals, or exhibit certain behaviors. Empowerment involves granting individuals the authority, autonomy, and resources to take control of their work and make decisions.

Motivated and empowered individuals are not only more productive but also more engaged and satisfied in their roles. The essence lies in recognizing that motivated and empowered teams contribute significantly to organizational success and innovation.

How to Motivate and Empower Effectively:

1. Recognize and Acknowledge Achievements:

Frequent recognition of individual and team achievements creates a positive and motivating work environment. Acknowledgment reinforces the value of contributions and encourages a culture of appreciation.

2. Provide Opportunities for Skill Development:

Empowerment is closely tied to skill development. Leaders can motivate and empower by offering opportunities for continuous learning and growth.

This can be through workshops, training programs, or mentorship initiatives.

3. Foster a Positive Work Culture:

A positive work culture, characterized by open communication, collaboration, and inclusivity, is a breeding ground for motivation and empowerment. Leaders set the tone by fostering a culture of respect and camaraderie.

4. Set Clear and Challenging Goals:

Motivation thrives when individuals have clear goals that challenge their capabilities. Leaders should collaboratively set SMART goals (Specific, Measurable, Achievable, Relevant, Time-bound) that align with both individual aspirations and organizational objectives.

5. Encourage Autonomy and Decision-Making:

Empowerment is realized through autonomy. Leaders empower their team by allowing individuals to make decisions within their scope of responsibility. This fosters a sense of ownership and accountability.

6. Provide Regular and Constructive Feedback:

Motivation is sustained through feedback. Leaders should provide regular, constructive feedback that recognizes achievements and guides individuals toward improvement. Feedback sessions should be a two-way dialogue, encouraging open communication.

7. Create a Recognition System:

Establishing a formal recognition system, such as employee of the month awards or peer recognition programs, adds a layer of external motivation. Recognizing and celebrating accomplishments reinforces a culture of appreciation.

When Motivation and Empowerment Are Most Effective:

1. During Times of Change:

Motivation is crucial during periods of change or uncertainty. Leaders who effectively communicate the purpose of change and empower individuals to navigate transitions foster resilience and adaptability.

2. With New Team Members:

Empowerment is especially important when onboarding new team members. Leaders should provide the necessary resources, guidance, and encouragement to help individuals integrate into the team and perform at their best.

3. Amidst Challenges:

Motivation and empowerment are tested during challenging times. Leaders who inspire confidence, offer support, and acknowledge efforts during adversity contribute to a resilient and motivated team.

4. Career Advancement Opportunities:

Motivation is heightened when individuals see a direct link between their efforts and career advancement. Leaders can empower team members by providing clarity on career paths and offering opportunities for advancement.

Key Takeaways:

- *Recognition Fosters Motivation:*

Frequent acknowledgment of achievements and contributions creates a motivating work environment.

- *Empowerment Thrives on Autonomy:*

Granting autonomy and decision-making authority empowers individuals to take control of their work and contribute meaningfully.

- *Positive Culture Nurtures Motivation and Empowerment:*

A positive work culture, characterized by open communication and inclusivity, serves as the foundation for motivation and empowerment.

- *Feedback Sustains Motivation:*

Regular, constructive feedback guides individuals toward improvement and sustains motivation over the long term.

- *Motivation and Empowerment Are Adaptable:*

Effective leaders recognize the adaptability of motivation and empowerment, applying these techniques during times of change, with new team members, in challenging situations, and amid career advancement opportunities.

In the grand tapestry of leadership, the techniques to motivate and empower emerge as the threads that weave together a culture of excellence. Leaders who master these techniques not only inspire individuals to reach their full potential but also lay the groundwork for a resilient and empowered organization poised for success.

Constructive Feedback and Performance Management

In the dynamic realm of leadership, the art of providing constructive feedback and effective performance management is paramount. This chapter delves into the intricacies of guiding individuals toward improvement, fostering growth, and maintaining a supportive framework through "Constructive Feedback and Performance Management."

Why Constructive Feedback and Performance Management Matter:

Constructive feedback involves providing specific, actionable insights to help individuals understand their strengths and areas for improvement. Performance management encompasses the processes and activities that ensure an individual or team's performance aligns with organizational objectives.

The essence lies in recognizing that feedback is not merely a critique but a tool for development. Performance management ensures that individual and collective efforts are directed toward achieving organizational goals.

How to Provide Constructive Feedback and Perform Effective Performance Management:

1. Establish Clear Expectations:

Before feedback can be given, it's crucial to establish clear expectations. Clearly defined roles, responsibilities, and performance metrics provide a foundation for effective feedback.

2. Timely and Regular Feedback:

Constructive feedback is most effective when it is provided in a timely manner. Regular check-ins, one-on-one sessions, and performance reviews offer opportunities for continuous improvement.

3. Be Specific and Actionable:

Feedback should be specific and actionable. Instead of vague statements, point out specific behaviors or achievements. Offer suggestions for improvement and provide a roadmap for achieving goals.

4. Encourage Self-Reflection:

Constructive feedback encourages individuals to reflect on their own performance. Leaders can guide this process by asking questions that prompt self-reflection, fostering a sense of ownership and accountability.

5. Acknowledge Achievements:

Performance management isn't solely about addressing areas for improvement. Acknowledge and celebrate achievements. Positive reinforcement boosts morale and motivates individuals to continue performing at their best.

6. Create a Development Plan:

Work collaboratively with individuals to create a development plan based on the feedback provided. This plan should outline specific goals, milestones, and the support needed to achieve them.

7. Provide Training and Resources:

Performance management involves ensuring that individuals have the necessary skills and resources to excel. Offer training programs, mentorship, or access to tools that facilitate professional development.

8. Use a 360-Degree Approach:

Gather feedback from multiple sources, including peers, subordinates, and self-assessments. A 360-degree approach provides a comprehensive view of an individual's performance and fosters a culture of openness.

When Constructive Feedback and Performance Management Are Most Effective:

1. During Regular Check-Ins:

Regular check-ins, whether formal or informal, are ideal times to provide constructive feedback. These sessions create a continuous feedback loop, allowing for real-time adjustments.

2. After Significant Projects or Milestones:

Performance management is particularly crucial after completing significant projects or reaching milestones. Reflecting on these experiences can uncover valuable insights for improvement.

3. *Amidst Periods of Change or Growth:*

During periods of organizational change or individual growth, feedback plays a pivotal role. It guides individuals through transitions, ensuring they adapt effectively and continue to contribute to the organization's success.

4. *In Addressing Performance Gaps:*

Constructive feedback is especially important when addressing performance gaps. Rather than punitive measures, a constructive approach identifies areas for improvement and provides the necessary support.

Key Takeaways:

- *Feedback as a Tool for Development:*

Constructive feedback is a powerful tool for individual and collective development, guiding individuals toward improvement and aligning efforts with organizational objectives.

- *Performance Management for Goal Alignment:*

Effective performance management ensures that individual and team efforts align with organizational goals, fostering a culture of continuous improvement.

- *Specificity and Actionability in Feedback:*

Constructive feedback should be specific, actionable, and focused on behaviors or achievements, providing individuals with clear guidance for improvement.

- *Encouraging Self-Reflection:*

Constructive feedback encourages self-reflection, fostering a sense of ownership and accountability for one's own performance.

- *360-Degree Approach to Feedback:*

A 360-degree feedback approach, incorporating insights from various sources, provides a holistic view of an individual's performance and encourages openness and collaboration.

In the leadership narrative, the ability to provide constructive feedback and effectively manage performance emerges as an art form that shapes not only individual growth but the overall success of the organization. Leaders who master this art create a culture where feedback is valued, improvement is continuous, and every individual is empowered to contribute their best to the collective journey of success.

Chapter 8: Team Building and Collaboration

Welcome to the heart of collaborative leadership in Chapter 8, "Team Building and Collaboration." As our narrative unfolds, this chapter is a deep dive into the pivotal elements that transform a group of individuals into a cohesive, high-performing team. Readers will navigate the intricacies of fostering collaboration, resolving conflicts, and achieving consensus—a triad of skills essential for any leader navigating the dynamic landscape of teamwork.

Upon completing this chapter, readers will gain insights into the fundamental principles and practices that underpin successful team dynamics. From building a high-performing team to fostering an environment where collaboration thrives, and finally, to resolving conflicts and reaching consensus, the journey through this chapter equips leaders with the tools necessary to steer their teams toward success.

1. Building a High-Performing Team:

Building a high-performing team involves strategically assembling individuals with complementary skills and fostering an environment that nurtures collaboration and excellence.

Key Takeaways:

- *Skill Assessment:* Identify and leverage individual strengths.
- *Clear Roles and Responsibilities:* Establish roles that align with team goals.
- *Communication:* Foster open and transparent communication.
- *Goal Alignment:* Ensure team goals align with organizational objectives.

- *Outcome:* Readers will discover the art of crafting a team that synergizes its collective strengths, propelling itself toward outstanding achievements.

2. Fostering a Collaborative Environment:

Fostering a collaborative environment goes beyond physical proximity; it involves creating a culture where ideas flow freely, and diverse perspectives are valued.

Key Takeaways:

- *Open Communication Channels:* Establish platforms for sharing ideas and feedback.
- *Inclusivity:* Encourage participation from all team members.
- *Celebrating Diversity:* Embrace diverse perspectives and backgrounds.
- *Shared Vision:* Ensure the team shares a common vision and purpose.

- *Outcome:* Readers will explore the strategies to cultivate an atmosphere where collaboration is not just encouraged but becomes an integral part of the team's DNA.

3. Conflict Resolution and Consensus Building:

Conflict resolution is the art of addressing disagreements constructively, while consensus building involves reaching collective decisions that all team members can support.

Key Takeaways:

- *Active Listening:* Hear all perspectives to understand the root of conflicts.
- *Mediation Skills:* Intervene and guide the resolution process when needed.
- *Common Ground Identification:* Find shared values to build consensus.

- *Decision-Making Processes:* Establish methods for reaching decisions agreeably.
- *Outcome:* Readers will emerge with the ability to navigate conflicts productively and guide their teams toward decisions that enjoy broad support.

Building a high-performing team involves recognizing and leveraging individual strengths to create a collective force that excels.

Fostering a collaborative environment is not just a strategy; it's a cultural shift where diversity is celebrated, and ideas flow seamlessly.

Conflict resolution skills are crucial for maintaining a healthy team dynamic. Leaders equipped with these skills can turn conflicts into opportunities for growth.

Consensus building is not about everyone getting their way but finding common ground. It ensures decisions are owned collectively, fostering commitment and accountability.

As leaders embark on this exploration of team building and collaboration, they will find themselves equipped with the knowledge and strategies to foster a high-performing team, nurture a collaborative environment, and deftly navigate conflicts toward consensus—a trio of skills essential for steering teams toward unprecedented success.

Building a High-Performing Team

Welcome to the intricacies of leadership where the alchemy of individuals transforms into the symphony of a high-performing team. This chapter delves into the essence of "Building a High-Performing Team," exploring the why, how, and when behind the formation of a collective force that not only meets but exceeds expectations.

Why Building a High-Performing Team Matters:

Building a high-performing team involves strategically assembling individuals with complementary skills, fostering an environment that nurtures collaboration, and aligning collective efforts with organizational objectives.

The essence lies in recognizing that a high-performing team is greater than the sum of its parts. It's a group that synergizes its collective strengths, propelling itself toward outstanding achievements and surpassing individual capabilities.

How to Build a High-Performing Team:

1. Skill Assessment:

Recognizing and leveraging individual strengths is foundational to team success.

Conduct a thorough assessment of team members' skills, experiences, and preferences. Identify complementary talents that, when combined, enhance the overall team capabilities.

2. Clear Roles and Responsibilities:

Ambiguity in roles leads to confusion and inefficiency.

Clearly define each team member's role, outlining their responsibilities and expectations. Ensure alignment with the team's overarching goals and the organization's mission.

3. *Communication:*

Open and transparent communication fosters a collaborative environment.

Establish regular communication channels, both formal and informal. Encourage team members to share ideas, concerns, and updates. Emphasize the importance of active listening to promote mutual understanding.

4. *Goal Alignment:*

Individual and team goals must align with organizational objectives.

Clearly articulate organizational goals and demonstrate how each team member's contributions contribute to these objectives. Foster a sense of shared purpose and highlight the collective impact of achieving common goals.

When Building a High-Performing Team Is Most Effective:

1. Formation of a New Team:

Lay a strong foundation for collaboration from the outset.

When a new team is formed, leaders have the opportunity to shape its culture, set expectations, and build a cohesive unit from the start.

2. During Periods of Change:

A high-performing team adapts effectively to change.

During organizational changes, such as restructuring or strategy shifts, building a high-performing team ensures resilience and adaptability.

3. *In Response to Challenges:*

Challenges require collective strength and collaboration.

When facing complex challenges, leaders can focus on building a high-performing team to harness diverse perspectives and skill sets.

Key Takeaways:

- *Synergizing Strengths Creates Excellence:* The synergy of diverse strengths is the cornerstone of high team performance.
- *Roles Provide Clarity:* Clear roles and responsibilities prevent confusion and enhance efficiency.

- ***Communication is the Lifeblood:*** Open and transparent communication is the lifeblood that sustains a collaborative environment.

- ***Alignment Fosters Purpose:*** Aligning individual and team goals with organizational objectives fosters a sense of purpose and shared commitment.

- ***Strategic Timing Enhances Impact:*** Building a high-performing team is strategically impactful during the formation of a new team, periods of change, and in response to challenges.

As leaders navigate the terrain of team building, understanding the intricacies of creating a high-performing team becomes a compass guiding them toward unprecedented achievements. This journey is not just about assembling a group of individuals but sculpting a collective force that rises to challenges, embraces change, and consistently delivers excellence.

Fostering a Collaborative Environment

Step into the realm of leadership where the threads of individual contributions weave a tapestry of collective achievement. This chapter unfolds the art and science of "Fostering a Collaborative Environment," exploring the profound impact of cultivating a workplace where ideas flow freely, diversity is celebrated, and collaboration becomes the heartbeat of success.

Why Fostering a Collaborative Environment Matters:

Fostering a collaborative environment goes beyond mere physical proximity; it involves creating a culture where ideas flow seamlessly, diverse perspectives are valued, and individuals feel empowered to contribute their unique strengths.

The essence lies in recognizing that collaboration is not just a strategy; it's a cultural shift—a commitment to openness, inclusivity, and the belief that collective intelligence surpasses individual brilliance.

How to Foster a Collaborative Environment:

1. Open Communication Channels:

Communication is the lifeblood of collaboration.

Establish diverse communication channels—regular team meetings, digital platforms, and informal gatherings. Encourage team members to share ideas, ask questions, and provide feedback openly.

2. Inclusivity:

Inclusive environments harness the power of diverse perspectives.

Actively seek and value contributions from all team members. Ensure that everyone has an opportunity to express their opinions, and create an atmosphere where diverse voices are heard and respected.

3. *Celebrating Diversity:*

Diverse teams drive innovation and problem-solving.

Acknowledge and celebrate the unique backgrounds, experiences, and perspectives of team members. Foster an environment where differences are seen as strengths that contribute to the richness of collaborative efforts.

4. *Shared Vision:*

A shared vision aligns individual efforts toward common goals.

Clearly articulate the organizational vision and how each team member's contributions contribute to that vision. This shared purpose becomes a unifying force, aligning the team's collective energy.

When Fostering a Collaborative Environment Is Most Effective:

1. *At the Onset of Team Formation:*

Lay the foundation for a collaborative culture from the beginning.

When a new team is formed, leaders have the unique opportunity to shape the team's culture and set expectations for collaboration.

2. *During Periods of Change:*

Collaboration enhances adaptability and resilience.

During organizational changes, fostering a collaborative environment ensures that teams can adapt effectively to new circumstances.

3. *In Times of Innovation and Creativity:*

Collaborative environments fuel innovation.

When creativity and innovation are crucial, a collaborative culture stimulates the sharing of ideas and the exploration of novel solutions.

Key Takeaways:

- ***Communication Fuels Collaboration:*** Open communication channels are the conduits through which collaboration flourishes.

- ***Inclusivity Drives Engagement:*** Inclusive environments engage all team members, unlocking the full potential of diverse perspectives.

- ***Diversity as a Strength:*** Celebrating diversity transforms differences into strengths that contribute to the team's collective success.

- ***A Shared Vision Unifies:*** A shared vision unifies individual efforts, aligning the team toward common goals.

- ***Strategic Timing Enhances Impact:*** Fostering a collaborative environment is strategically impactful during the formation of a new team, periods of change, and in times of innovation and creativity.

As leaders navigate the landscape of collaborative leadership, the understanding that collaboration is not just a methodology but a way of being becomes paramount. This journey is an exploration of cultural shifts, where openness, inclusivity, and shared purpose converge to create an environment where collaboration is not just a practice—it's the very essence of success.

Conflict Resolution and Consensus Building

Embark on a journey through the delicate yet transformative landscapes of leadership. In this chapter, "Conflict Resolution and Consensus Building," we unravel the intricacies of managing conflicts constructively and forging collective decisions that garner broad support. This exploration navigates the why, how, and when behind conflict resolution and consensus building, essential skills for leaders steering their teams toward harmonious collaboration.

Why Conflict Resolution and Consensus Building Matter:

Conflict resolution involves addressing disagreements in a constructive manner, while consensus building is the process of reaching collective decisions that all team members can support.

The essence lies in recognizing that conflicts, when navigated effectively, become opportunities for growth, and consensus building fosters a sense of collective ownership and commitment.

How to Resolve Conflicts and Build Consensus:

1. Active Listening:

Understanding precedes resolution.

Encourage active listening during conflicts. Ensure all parties have the opportunity to express their perspectives without interruption. This lays the groundwork for empathetic understanding.

2. Mediation Skills:

Leaders play a crucial role in guiding resolution.

Develop mediation skills to facilitate open and constructive dialogue. Intervene when necessary, asking probing questions that lead parties toward mutually beneficial solutions.

3. *Common Ground Identification:*

Common ground forms the foundation for consensus.

Identify shared values, goals, or interests during discussions. Emphasize these commonalities to create a platform for collaborative decision-making.

4. *Decision-Making Processes:*

Structured processes enhance clarity.

Establish clear decision-making processes that outline how consensus will be reached. This might include voting, discussion rounds, or other collaborative methods that ensure everyone's input is considered.

When Conflict Resolution and Consensus Building Are Most Effective:

1. *During Regular Check-Ins:*

Nipping conflicts in the bud prevents escalation.

Regular check-ins create a continuous feedback loop, allowing for the timely resolution of emerging conflicts.

2. *After Significant Projects or Milestones:*

Reflection uncovers insights for improvement.

Post-project reviews provide opportunities to address conflicts and identify lessons for future consensus building.

3. *Amidst Periods of Change or Growth:*

Adaptability requires collective understanding.

During periods of change or growth, resolving conflicts and building consensus ensures the team can adapt effectively to new circumstances.

Key Takeaways:

- ***Conflict as Growth Opportunity:*** Resolving conflicts transforms challenges into opportunities for growth and improvement.

- ***Leaders as Guides in Resolution:*** Leaders play a crucial role as mediators, guiding parties toward constructive dialogue and resolution.

- ***Common Ground Fosters Consensus:*** Identifying common ground is the cornerstone of consensus building, fostering a sense of shared purpose.

- ***Structured Processes Enhance Decision-Making:*** Clear decision-making processes enhance the efficiency and transparency of consensus building.

- ***Strategic Timing for Effectiveness:*** Conflict resolution is most effective during regular check-ins, after significant projects, and amidst periods of change or growth.

In the orchestra of leadership, conflict resolution and consensus building emerge as the conductors, guiding the symphony of collaboration. This chapter invites leaders to recognize conflicts not as disruptions but as opportunities for growth. Through empathetic listening, skilled mediation, and the identification of common ground, leaders can resolve conflicts constructively and build consensus that unifies teams toward collective success.

Part III:

Continual Growth and Adaptation

Chapter 9: The Learning Leader

Step into the realm of leadership evolution in Chapter 9, "The Learning Leader." This chapter is a compass guiding leader toward a mindset of perpetual growth, emphasizing the profound impact of continuous learning, the establishment of a learning culture, and the transformative potential inherent in failures and mistakes. As we unravel the narrative of "The Learning Leader," readers will discover the essence of leadership as an ever-evolving journey marked by curiosity, adaptability, and a commitment to learning from every experience.

Upon completing this chapter, readers will have gleaned insights into the pivotal role of continuous learning in leadership. They will understand the dynamics of building a learning culture within their teams and harnessing the invaluable lessons embedded in failures and mistakes. "The Learning Leader" is not just a concept; it's a call to action—a roadmap for leaders to cultivate an environment where growth is constant, innovation is nurtured, and setbacks become stepping stones to success.

1.The Importance of Continuous Learning:

In this section, readers will explore the dynamic concept of continuous learning in leadership. It transcends the traditional view of education, emphasizing the importance of curiosity, adaptability, and personalized learning plans. The outcome is a deep understanding of how continuous learning enhances leadership effectiveness and resilience.

2. Building a Learning Culture:

The exploration continues with the concept of building a learning culture within organizations. Leaders are called to exemplify a commitment to learning, fostering collaborative platforms, and recognizing individual and collective learning achievements. This sub-chapter unveils the transformative power of organizational culture in shaping innovation and adaptability.

3. Leveraging Failures and Mistakes as Learning Opportunities:

The final sub-chapter challenges conventional views on failures and mistakes. It encourages leaders to see setbacks not as impediments but as stepping stones to success. By introducing reflection practices, destigmatizing failure, and implementing lessons learned, leaders can leverage setbacks as invaluable sources of learning, innovation, and continuous improvement.

Key Takeaways:

- ***Leadership as a Continuous Journey:*** The learning leader understands that leadership is not a destination but a continuous journey marked by curiosity and adaptability.

- ***Cultivating a Learning Culture:*** Building a learning culture requires leadership example, collaborative platforms, and recognition of learning achievements to foster innovation and adaptability.

- ***Failures as Stepping Stones:*** A learning leader sees failures and mistakes not as setbacks but as opportunities for reflection, growth, and continuous improvement.

- ***Transformation Through Learning:*** Continuous learning, a learning culture, and the ability to leverage failures collectively contribute to the transformative potential of a learning leader.

"The Learning Leader" is an exploration of leadership as a dynamic and ever-evolving journey. As readers navigate through the importance of continuous learning, the creation of a learning culture, and the art of leveraging failures, they will emerge not only as leaders but as architects of growth and innovation. This chapter serves as an invitation for leaders to embrace the mindset of a perpetual learner, shaping not only their own trajectories but also the cultures and successes of the teams they lead.

The Importance of Continuous Learning

In the ever-evolving landscape of leadership, a cornerstone principle reigns supreme—the importance of continuous learning. This chapter unfurls the profound significance of perpetually acquiring knowledge, skills, and insights throughout one's leadership journey. We embark on a journey into the essence of continuous learning, exploring the why, the how, and the transformative power it wields in shaping leaders into adaptable, innovative, and resilient individuals.

The Definition of Continuous Learning:

Continuous learning transcends traditional notions of education. It is a dynamic process wherein leaders commit to ongoing personal and professional development. It involves a proactive and intentional approach to acquiring new knowledge, refining existing skills, and staying abreast of industry trends and innovations. A continuous learner is driven by curiosity, embracing learning not as a task but as a fundamental aspect of leadership.

The Why of Continuous Learning:

1. *Curiosity as a Catalyst:*

A continuous learner is propelled by an insatiable curiosity. This innate desire to understand, explore, and question fuels a leader's growth. Curiosity transforms challenges into opportunities, prompting leaders to seek knowledge beyond immediate needs, fostering a mindset of exploration and discovery.

2. *Adaptability as a Core Competency:*

The pace of change in today's world demands leaders who can adapt swiftly. Continuous learning equips leaders with the agility needed to navigate evolving landscapes. Adaptable leaders embrace new technologies, management methodologies, and industry shifts, positioning themselves as stalwarts in an ever-shifting environment.

3. Personal Development Plans:

Continuous learning thrives when guided by personalized plans. Leaders craft these plans based on self-assessment, identifying areas for growth aligned with professional goals. Such plans become roadmaps, ensuring that learning efforts are strategic, purposeful, and tailored to individual aspirations.

The How of Continuous Learning:

1. Embracing Diverse Learning Channels:

Leaders must diversify their learning channels, tapping into a wealth of resources. This includes formal education, workshops, seminars, online courses, and informal avenues like podcasts, industry publications, and mentorship programs. A varied approach ensures exposure to a broad spectrum of insights.

2. *Networking and Collaborative Learning:*

Learning extends beyond individual endeavors. Leaders are encouraged to engage in networking and collaborative learning. Interacting with peers, industry experts, and professionals from diverse backgrounds fosters the exchange of ideas, perspectives, and best practices.

3. *Reflective Practices:*

Integral to continuous learning is the art of reflection. Leaders must engage in introspection, analyzing their experiences, successes, and setbacks. Reflection cultivates self-awareness, allowing leaders to extract lessons from their journeys and apply them to future endeavors.

The Transformative Outcome:

Continuous learning begets transformative outcomes for leaders:

- ***Enhanced Leadership Effectiveness:*** Leaders who embrace continuous learning are equipped with the latest knowledge and skills, enhancing their decision-making and problem-solving abilities.

- ***Increased Adaptability and Resilience:*** Continuous learners exhibit heightened adaptability, thriving in environments characterized by change and uncertainty. They become resilient leaders capable of navigating challenges with poise.

- ***Staying Ahead of Industry Trends:*** In rapidly evolving industries, continuous learners stay ahead of the curve. They anticipate trends, innovate, and position their teams or organizations as industry frontrunners.

"The Importance of Continuous Learning" is a testament to the dynamic nature of leadership. In an era where change is constant, leaders who commit to continuous learning are the torchbearers of progress. This chapter encourages leaders to cultivate a mindset of perpetual curiosity, adaptability, and intentional growth. As they embrace the transformative power of continuous learning, leaders not only enrich their own journeys but also elevate the trajectory of their teams and organizations in an ever-evolving landscape.

Building a Learning Culture

In the intricate tapestry of leadership, the concept of "Building a Learning Culture" emerges as a linchpin for organizational success. This chapter delves into the profound significance of fostering an environment where curiosity thrives, collaboration is embraced, and continuous improvement becomes ingrained in the organizational DNA. As we unravel the layers of building a learning culture, we explore the definitions, essential steps, and the transformative impact it has on organizations and their leaders.

The Definition of a Learning Culture:

A learning culture is not merely a set of training programs or workshops; it is a pervasive mindset within an organization that values continuous learning, knowledge-sharing, and innovation. In a learning culture, every interaction becomes an opportunity for growth, and the collective pursuit of knowledge is woven into the fabric of daily operations.

The Why of Building a Learning Culture:

1. *Innovation and Adaptability:*

A learning culture is a crucible for innovation and adaptability. It encourages teams to explore new ideas, experiment with different approaches, and adapt swiftly to changes in the business landscape. Innovation becomes a collective endeavor, and adaptability becomes second nature.

2. *Employee Engagement and Satisfaction:*

Organizations with a strong learning culture tend to have higher levels of employee engagement and satisfaction. When employees perceive that their growth and development are prioritized, they are more likely to be invested in their work, contributing positively to the organization's overall success.

3. Attracting and Retaining Talent:

In a competitive job market, a learning culture serves as a powerful magnet for talent. Potential employees are drawn to organizations that prioritize their professional development. Moreover, organizations with a reputation for fostering learning are better positioned to retain their top talent.

The How of Building a Learning Culture:

1. Leadership Example:

Leadership sets the tone for a learning culture. Leaders must exemplify a commitment to continuous learning, showcasing their curiosity, embracing new ideas, and actively participating in learning initiatives. When leaders embody a learning mindset, it permeates throughout the organization.

2. Collaborative Learning Platforms:

Establishing platforms for collaborative learning is pivotal. This includes formal mechanisms like workshops, seminars, and training programs, as well as informal channels such as knowledge-sharing sessions, mentorship programs, and peer-to-peer learning. These platforms encourage the exchange of ideas and insights.

3. Recognition of Learning Achievements:

Recognizing and celebrating individual and collective learning achievements is essential. Acknowledging milestones, certifications, and contributions to the learning culture creates a positive feedback loop. It reinforces the value placed on continuous improvement and motivates others to actively engage in learning.

The Transformative Impact:

1. Enhanced Organizational Agility:

Organizations with a robust learning culture exhibit enhanced agility. They can pivot quickly in response to industry trends, technological advancements, and changing customer needs. This adaptability positions them as leaders in dynamic and competitive markets.

2. Increased Innovation and Creativity:

A learning culture nurtures innovation and creativity. When employees are encouraged to explore, take risks, and learn from failures, they become catalysts for inventive solutions. Creativity flourishes in an environment where learning is not confined but celebrated.

3. Continuous Improvement in Performance:

The pursuit of excellence is inherent in a learning culture. Teams and individuals are driven to continuously improve their performance. This leads to a cycle of refinement, where processes, products, and services are iteratively enhanced.

Overcoming Challenges:

- ***Resistance to Change:*** Building a learning culture may encounter resistance, especially if the organization has a history of rigid structures. Addressing this requires effective communication, emphasizing the benefits of a learning culture, and showcasing success stories.

- ***Resource Constraints:*** Limited resources can pose challenges. However, a learning culture doesn't necessarily require extensive financial investments. Leveraging existing resources creatively, such as internal expertise and collaborative platforms, can mitigate resource constraints.

"Building a Learning Culture" is a journey that transforms organizations into vibrant, adaptive, and innovative entities. As leaders cultivate an environment where learning is not an isolated event but a continual process, they lay the groundwork for sustained success. This chapter serves as a guide for leaders to champion a learning culture—fostering curiosity, collaboration, and a collective commitment to continuous improvement. As organizations embrace this paradigm shift, they position themselves not only as industry leaders but as hubs of innovation and growth in an ever-evolving landscape.

Leveraging Failures and Mistakes as Learning Opportunities

In the dynamic realm of leadership, the ability to "Leverage Failures and Mistakes as Learning Opportunities" stands as a testament to resilience, growth, and innovation. This chapter embarks on an exploration of the profound importance of viewing setbacks not as stumbling blocks but as stepping stones toward continuous improvement. We delve into the definitions, delve into the steps, and unveil the transformative power of leveraging failures and mistakes as invaluable sources of learning.

Leveraging failures and mistakes as learning opportunities involves a mindset shift—from viewing setbacks as roadblocks to embracing them as catalysts for growth. It's a strategic approach to extracting insights from failures, applying those lessons to future endeavors, and fostering a culture where learning from mistakes is not just encouraged but celebrated.

The Why of Leveraging Failures:

1. Promoting Innovation:

Failure is often a byproduct of experimentation and risk-taking—the cornerstones of innovation. Embracing failures as learning opportunities creates an environment where individuals are encouraged to push boundaries, explore new ideas, and contribute to a culture of continuous innovation.

2. Cultivating Resilience:

Leaders and teams that can navigate failures with resilience become better equipped to face future challenges. The ability to bounce back from setbacks, armed with newfound insights, fosters a culture of adaptability and perseverance.

3. *Driving Continuous Improvement:*

Failures, when analyzed and understood, become powerful drivers of continuous improvement. They unveil areas for refinement, highlight potential weaknesses, and pave the way for strategic enhancements in processes, strategies, and decision-making.

The How of Leveraging Failures:

1. *Reflection Practices:*

Establishing reflective practices is integral to leveraging failures effectively. After a setback, individuals and teams should engage in structured reflection, examining the circumstances, decisions, and contributing factors. This introspective process helps unearth valuable insights.

2. *De-stigmatization of Failure:*

Fostering a culture where failure is destigmatized is crucial. When mistakes are viewed not as shameful missteps but as integral parts of the learning journey, individuals are more likely to share their experiences openly, facilitating collective learning.

3. Implementation of Lessons Learned:

Extracting lessons from failures is transformative only when those insights are actively implemented. Leaders and teams should develop actionable strategies to integrate newfound knowledge into their processes, strategies, and decision-making frameworks.

The Transformative Impact:

1. Fostering a Growth Mindset:

Leveraging failures nurtures a growth mindset—a belief that abilities and intelligence can be developed through dedication and hard work. Individuals with a growth mindset view failures not as indictments of their capabilities but as opportunities for improvement.

2. Enhancing Decision-Making:

Leaders who learn from failures develop a nuanced understanding of risk and decision-making. They become adept at assessing potential pitfalls, making informed choices, and navigating uncertainty with a heightened sense of foresight.

3. Catalyzing Innovation and Creativity:

Organizations that embrace failure as a companion to innovation and creativity witness a surge in groundbreaking ideas. When the fear of failure is mitigated, individuals are more willing to experiment, explore unconventional solutions, and contribute to a culture of innovation.

Overcoming Challenges:

- ***Cultural Resistance:*** Some organizational cultures may resist the idea of openly acknowledging and learning from failures. Overcoming this challenge requires a strategic communication effort, leadership commitment, and showcasing success stories that emerged from setbacks.

- ***Fear of Repercussions:*** Individuals may hesitate to admit mistakes due to a fear of negative consequences. Building a culture that emphasizes learning over blame, where mistakes are seen as opportunities for growth, can help mitigate this fear.

"Leveraging Failures and Mistakes as Learning Opportunities" is a paradigm shift in how setbacks are perceived within the tapestry of leadership. It is an invitation to view failures not as signals of defeat but as guides on the path to success. This chapter serves as a compass for leaders and teams, guiding them through the process of reflective practices, the de-stigmatization of failure, and the active implementation of lessons learned. As organizations cultivate a culture that embraces failures as integral components of the learning journey, they position themselves not just for recovery but for transformation and continuous advancement in an ever-evolving landscape.

Chapter 10: Embracing Change and Innovation

"Embracing Change and Innovation," the pivotal Chapter 10 of our journey, delves into the dynamic intersection of leadership, change, and innovation. In this transformative chapter, readers will unravel the intricacies of navigating change, fostering innovation, and overcoming resistance. The sub-chapters—The Role of Leadership in Driving Change, Leading Innovative Teams, and Overcoming Resistance to Change—form a comprehensive exploration that transcends theory, offering actionable insights for leaders navigating the evolving landscape of their organizations.

Upon completing Chapter 10, readers will gain a profound understanding of:

1. The Role of Leadership in Driving Change:

- Leadership Dynamics: Explore the integral role leadership plays in steering organizational change.

- Strategic Leadership: Understand how leaders strategically drive change initiatives, aligning them with the organizational vision.

- Communication Strategies: Uncover effective communication strategies leaders employ to convey the need for change and garner support.

2. Leading Innovative Teams:

- Team Dynamics: Delve into the dynamics of leading teams through the innovative process.

- Cultivating a Creative Environment: Learn how leaders foster an environment that stimulates creativity and innovation.

- Empowering Teams: Understand the empowerment strategies leaders use to encourage team members to contribute their innovative ideas.

3. *Overcoming Resistance to Change:*

- Understanding Resistance: Explore the psychology behind resistance to change and how leaders can decipher its root causes.

- Change Management Strategies: Uncover effective change management strategies leaders employ to address and mitigate resistance.

- Cultivating a Change-Ready Culture: Learn how leaders cultivate organizational cultures that embrace change, minimizing resistance.

❖ **Why You Need to Read This Chapter:**

1. ***Navigating Leadership Challenges:*** In the ever-evolving landscape of organizational leadership, change is a constant. This chapter equips leaders with the insights and strategies needed to navigate the complexities of change, fostering adaptability and resilience.

2. ***Driving Innovation for Success:*** Innovation is the lifeblood of organizational success. Readers will discover how effective leadership drives innovation, empowering teams to explore novel solutions and position the organization as a frontrunner in their industry.

3. ***Mitigating Resistance for Sustainable Change:*** Resistance to change can be a formidable barrier. This chapter provides leaders with the tools to understand, address, and mitigate resistance, creating a culture where change is not just accepted but embraced.

❖ **Who Will Benefit:**

- Leaders and Executives: This chapter is a guide for leaders at all levels, providing strategies to lead their teams through change and cultivate innovation.

- Managers and Team Leads: Those responsible for leading teams will find actionable insights on fostering creativity, empowering team members, and managing resistance.

- Change Management Practitioners: Professionals specializing in change management will discover new perspectives and strategies to enhance their approaches.

- Organizational Development Professionals: Those focused on fostering organizational growth and development will find valuable insights to drive positive change.

❖ **The Role of Leadership in Driving Change:**

In the dynamic landscape of organizational evolution, leadership stands as the linchpin for driving change. This sub-chapter unveils the multifaceted role leaders play in instigating and steering change initiatives.

- ***Leadership Dynamics:*** Explore the key dynamics that make leadership pivotal in change management. Understand the qualities that transform leaders into effective change agents.

- ***Vision Alignment:*** Delve into the art of aligning change initiatives with the overarching vision of the organization. Examine case studies and practical strategies for ensuring seamless integration of change with the organizational vision.

- ***Communication Strategies:*** Uncover effective communication strategies employed by successful leaders to convey the imperative for change. Learn how to craft compelling narratives that resonate with diverse stakeholders, fostering understanding and garnering support.

❖ **Leading Innovative Teams:**

This sub-chapter immerses readers into the intricacies of leading teams through the creative and innovative process, unlocking the potential for groundbreaking ideas.

- *Team Dynamics:* Delve into the dynamics that characterize innovative teams. Explore the synergy between leadership and team members in fostering a culture of creativity and exploration.

- *Cultivating a Creative Environment:* Learn how leaders create environments that stimulate creativity and innovation. Understand the role of physical spaces, organizational culture, and leadership behaviors in cultivating creativity.

- ***Empowering Teams:*** Uncover strategies leaders use to empower team members, encouraging them to contribute and implement innovative ideas. Case studies and real-world examples illustrate successful empowerment initiatives.

❖ **Overcoming Resistance to Change:**

Resistance to change is a common challenge, and this sub-chapter equips leaders with the insights and strategies needed to address and mitigate resistance effectively.

- ***Understanding Resistance:*** Explore the psychology behind resistance to change. Gain insights into the various forms of resistance and how they manifest at individual and organizational levels.

- ***Change Management Strategies:*** Uncover effective change management strategies employed by leaders to address and mitigate resistance. Learn how to develop and implement comprehensive change management plans that anticipate and navigate resistance.

- ***Cultivating a Change-Ready Culture:*** Discover how leaders cultivate organizational cultures that embrace change, minimizing resistance. Understand the long-term strategies for embedding a change-ready mindset into the fabric of the organization.

These sub-chapters collectively serve as a comprehensive guide for leaders navigating the complexities of change and innovation. Readers will emerge with a nuanced understanding of the leadership dynamics in change management, the intricacies of leading innovative teams, and effective strategies for overcoming resistance. By mastering these facets, leaders can steer their organizations toward a future marked by adaptability, creativity, and sustained success.

"Embracing Change and Innovation" isn't just a chapter; it's a roadmap for leaders navigating the evolving landscapes of leadership. In a world where change is constant and innovation is a necessity, this chapter empowers leaders to not only adapt but to thrive. It's an invitation to embrace change as a catalyst for growth, lead teams through innovation, and overcome resistance with strategic finesse. Whether you're a seasoned executive or an emerging leader, this chapter offers the insights you need to steer your organization toward a future marked by adaptability, innovation, and sustained success.

The Role of Leadership in Driving Change

In the ever-evolving landscape of organizational dynamics, the role of leadership in driving change is pivotal. This chapter unravels the complexities and nuances of leadership's function in instigating and steering change initiatives. From understanding leadership dynamics to aligning change with the organizational vision and employing effective communication strategies, each facet contributes to a holistic comprehension of the leader's role in navigating the transformative journey of change.

The role of leadership in driving change encompasses the strategic and influential actions undertaken by leaders to initiate, guide, and sustain organizational change. It involves creating a vision for the future, aligning stakeholders with this vision, and navigating the challenges inherent in transforming established norms and practices.

❖ **Leadership Dynamics:**

1. ***Visionary Leadership:*** Visionary leaders articulate a compelling vision that serves as the driving force behind change initiatives. They inspire and motivate teams by providing a clear picture of the desired future state.

2. ***Strategic Thinking:*** Effective leaders engage in strategic thinking, assessing the current state of the organization and envisioning the steps required for successful change. They formulate plans that align with organizational goals and anticipate potential obstacles.

3. ***Adaptive Leadership:*** Leaders must be adaptive, responsive to changing circumstances, and capable of adjusting strategies as the change journey unfolds. The ability to navigate

uncertainties and learn from feedback is integral to adaptive leadership.

❖ **Steps in Driving Change:**

1. ***Assessment and Analysis:*** Leaders conduct a thorough assessment of the organization's current state, identifying areas requiring change. Analysis involves understanding the impact of proposed changes on various stakeholders.

2. ***Creating a Compelling Vision:*** Visionary leaders craft a compelling vision that communicates the benefits and necessity of change. The vision serves as a guiding beacon, inspiring commitment and engagement.

3. ***Building a Coalition:*** Leaders cultivate a coalition of key influencers and stakeholders who champion the change. Collaboration and

consensus-building are crucial in garnering support.

4. ***Effective Communication:*** Communication is a linchpin in the change process. Leaders employ transparent and persuasive communication strategies. Regular updates, town hall meetings, and open forums foster a culture of transparency and inclusivity.

5. ***Resource Allocation:*** Leaders allocate resources strategically, ensuring that the change initiative is adequately supported. This includes financial resources, skilled personnel, and technological infrastructure.

6. ***Implementation and Monitoring:*** The execution phase involves implementing the planned changes systematically. Leaders monitor progress, addressing challenges promptly and ensuring alignment with the established vision.

7. ***Feedback and Adaptation:*** A feedback loop is crucial for continuous improvement. Leaders gather feedback from stakeholders and make necessary adjustments. Adaptive leadership involves a willingness to revise strategies based on insights gained during the change process.

❖ **Challenges and Solutions:**

1. **Resistance to Change:**

   - *Challenge:* Resistance is a common barrier in change initiatives.

   - *Solution:* Leaders proactively address concerns, communicate the benefits, and involve resistant individuals in the change process.

2. **Lack of Clarity:**

   - *Challenge:* Ambiguity and lack of clarity can lead to confusion.

- *Solution:* Leaders provide clear communication, define roles, and offer guidance to mitigate uncertainties.

3. **Organizational Culture Clash:**

- *Challenge:* Existing organizational culture may clash with the proposed changes.

- *Solution:* Leaders work on aligning the change with the existing culture or gradually shifting cultural norms to accommodate the change.

The role of leadership in driving change is an intricate dance of vision, strategy, and adaptability. Effective leaders navigate the complexities by fostering a culture of transparency, inspiring commitment, and strategically implementing change initiatives. By understanding the dynamics of leadership in change, organizations can not only weather transformations but emerge stronger, more agile, and poised for sustained success. This chapter serves as a guide for leaders navigating the change landscape, offering insights and strategies to propel their organizations into a future marked by adaptability and innovation.

Leading Innovative Teams

In the ever-evolving landscape of modern organizations, leading innovative teams has become a cornerstone of success. This chapter explores the intricacies of guiding teams through the creative and innovative process. From understanding team dynamics to cultivating a creative environment and empowering teams, each element contributes to a comprehensive understanding of the leader's role in fostering innovation.

Leading innovative teams involves the deliberate and strategic guidance of a group towards creative problem-solving, ideation, and the generation of groundbreaking ideas. It's about creating an environment where team members are empowered to think outside the box, collaborate effectively, and contribute their unique perspectives to drive innovation.

❖ **Team Dynamics:**

1. ***Collaborative Culture:*** Innovative teams thrive in a collaborative culture where open communication and idea-sharing are encouraged. Leaders foster an environment where team members feel comfortable expressing their thoughts without fear of judgment.

2. ***Diversity and Inclusion:*** Teams benefit from diverse perspectives. Leaders actively seek diversity in skills, backgrounds, and experiences within their teams. Inclusive leadership ensures that every team member feels valued and heard, promoting a rich tapestry of ideas.

3. ***Dynamic Leadership:*** Leaders of innovative teams embrace a dynamic leadership style. They adapt to the evolving needs of the team and the creative process. Empowering leadership involves providing guidance while

allowing team members the autonomy to explore and experiment.

❖ **Cultivating a Creative Environment:**

1. ***Physical Space Design:*** The physical workspace significantly influences creativity. Leaders design spaces that encourage collaboration, feature flexible work areas, and inspire creativity. Thoughtful office layouts and conducive environments foster a culture of innovation.

2. ***Organizational Culture:*** The overall organizational culture sets the tone for creativity. Leaders actively shape a culture that values experimentation, risk-taking, and learning from failures. A culture that celebrates creativity as a core value attracts and retains innovative talent.

3. ***Resources for Innovation:*** Providing resources, whether financial, technological, or educational, is crucial for fostering innovation. Leaders allocate budgets, invest in training, and ensure access to tools that support the creative process.

❖ **Empowering Teams:**

1. ***Encouraging Idea Generation:*** Leaders empower teams by actively encouraging the generation of ideas. Regular brainstorming sessions and idea-sharing forums create a culture of continuous innovation. Recognition of individual and team contributions reinforces the value placed on creative thinking.

2. ***Autonomy and Ownership:*** Innovative teams thrive when members have a sense of ownership over their work. Leaders provide autonomy, allowing team members to take

charge of their projects. Ownership fosters a commitment to success and a willingness to go above and beyond.

3. ***Continuous Learning and Development:*** Leaders invest in the continuous learning and development of team members. Training programs, workshops, and opportunities for skill enhancement contribute to a culture of growth. A commitment to professional development creates a team of adaptable and forward-thinking individuals.

❖ **Steps in Leading Innovative Teams:**

1. ***Define Clear Objectives:*** Leaders set clear objectives for the team, aligning them with the organization's overall goals. Clear objectives provide a roadmap for the team's innovative efforts.

2. ***Build a Diverse Team:*** Leaders intentionally assemble teams with diverse skills, backgrounds, and perspectives. Diversity sparks creativity and ensures a broad range of ideas are considered.

3. ***Foster Open Communication:*** Effective communication is paramount. Leaders create channels for open and transparent communication within the team. Open dialogue encourages the free flow of ideas and constructive feedback.

4. ***Provide Resources:*** Leaders ensure that teams have the necessary resources, whether financial, technological, or human, to support their innovative endeavors. Adequate resources empower teams to turn ideas into actionable projects.

5. ***Promote a Growth Mindset:*** Leaders cultivate a growth mindset within the team,

emphasizing the potential for development and learning from challenges. A growth mindset encourages resilience and a positive approach to overcoming obstacles.

6. *Celebrate Achievements:* Acknowledging and celebrating both small and significant achievements reinforces the value of innovative contributions. Recognition boosts morale and motivates teams to sustain their innovative efforts.

❖ **Overcoming Challenges:**

1. **Fear of Failure:**

- *Challenge:* Team members may fear failure, inhibiting their willingness to take risks.

- *Solution:* Leaders destigmatize failure, emphasizing its role in the learning process and showcasing examples where failures led to eventual success.

2. **Lack of Time for Creativity:**

- Challenge: Teams may feel overwhelmed by tight deadlines, leaving little time for creative exploration.
- Solution: Leaders allocate dedicated time for brainstorming and creativity, recognizing the long-term benefits of innovation.

3. **Resistance to Change:**

- Challenge: Existing processes or team members may resist innovative changes.
- Solution: Leaders communicate the necessity of innovation, addressing concerns and providing a clear rationale for change.

Leading innovative teams is a dynamic and multifaceted role that requires a combination of visionary leadership, a commitment to fostering a creative environment, and the empowerment of team members. Successful leaders in this realm understand the nuances of team dynamics, the importance of cultivating a culture of innovation, and the strategies for overcoming challenges. By mastering the art of leading innovative teams, organizations not only stay ahead in a rapidly changing world but also become hubs of creativity, driving sustained success and growth. This chapter serves as a comprehensive guide for leaders aspiring to harness the power of innovation within their teams and organizations.

Overcoming Resistance to Change

In the journey of organizational transformation, overcoming resistance to change stands as a pivotal challenge. This chapter delves into the intricacies of understanding, addressing, and ultimately overcoming resistance within the organizational context. From decoding the psychology of resistance to implementing effective change management strategies and cultivating a change-ready culture, each aspect contributes to a comprehensive guide for leaders navigating the turbulent waters of change.

Resistance to change refers to the reluctance or opposition displayed by individuals or groups within an organization when faced with alterations to established processes, structures, or cultural norms. It's a natural response rooted in the fear of the unknown, the comfort of familiarity, and the potential disruptions change might bring.

❖ **Understanding Resistance:**

1. ***Psychology of Resistance:*** Resistance often stems from fear, uncertainty, and a perceived loss of control. Understanding the psychological factors at play is crucial for leaders seeking to address resistance effectively.

2. ***Identifying Root Causes:*** Leaders must delve into the specific reasons behind resistance. Common causes include fear of job loss, perceived lack of benefits, or a belief that the current state is preferable.

3. ***Levels of Resistance:*** Resistance can manifest at different levels, from individual employees to entire departments. Recognizing the scope of resistance helps tailor interventions appropriately.

❖ **Steps in Overcoming Resistance:**

1. *Communication and Transparency:* Open and transparent communication is the cornerstone of overcoming resistance. Leaders articulate the reasons for change, the envisioned benefits, and address concerns directly.

2. *Involvement and Participation:* Involving employees in the change process fosters a sense of ownership. Participation empowers individuals to contribute ideas, reducing the fear associated with imposed changes.

3. *Education and Training:* Providing education on the necessity of change and offering training programs equips individuals with the skills needed for the new paradigm. Education mitigates uncertainty and builds confidence in navigating the upcoming changes.

4. ***Addressing Individual Concerns:*** Leaders address individual concerns through one-on-one discussions. Tailoring communication to address specific fears or doubts builds trust and reduces resistance.

5. ***Showcasing Success Stories:*** Highlighting successful examples of change within the organization serves as a powerful motivational tool. Success stories create a positive narrative and inspire confidence in the change process.

6. ***Change Champions:*** Identifying and empowering change champions within the organization is instrumental. These individuals, enthusiastic about the change, can influence their peers positively.

❖ **Change Management Strategies:**

1. ***Clear Vision and Goals:*** A clear vision and well-defined goals provide a roadmap for the

change journey. Clarity helps individuals understand the purpose and anticipated outcomes of the change.

2. ***Incremental Changes:*** Implementing change incrementally reduces the shock factor. Small, manageable changes allow individuals to adapt gradually, minimizing resistance.

3. ***Feedback Mechanisms:*** Establishing feedback mechanisms creates a channel for individuals to express concerns. Leaders use feedback to refine the change strategy and address emerging issues.

4. ***Flexible Approach:*** Leaders adopt a flexible approach, acknowledging that adjustments may be necessary. Flexibility demonstrates responsiveness to feedback and a commitment to the well-being of the organization and its members.

- ❖ **Cultivating a Change-Ready Culture:**

    1. ***Leadership Commitment:*** Leadership commitment to change is contagious. When leaders demonstrate a wholehearted dedication to the change process, it sets the tone for the entire organization.

    2. ***Communication of Benefits:*** Continually communicating the benefits of change reinforces its positive aspects. Understanding the advantages encourages individuals to see change as an opportunity rather than a threat.

    3. ***Recognition of Contributions:*** Recognizing and appreciating the contributions of those embracing change creates a culture of positivity. Acknowledgment reinforces the importance of individual efforts in the collective journey.

- ❖ **Overcoming Challenges:**

1. **Lack of Leadership Support:**

- Challenge: Resistance intensifies when leaders are perceived as unsupportive.
- Solution: Leaders actively demonstrate their commitment to change, providing visible support and guidance.

2. Unclear Communication:

- Challenge: Ambiguous or unclear communication breeds confusion and resistance.
- Solution: Leaders prioritize clear and consistent communication, ensuring that everyone understands the reasons behind the change.

3. Inadequate Training:

- Challenge: Lack of training can leave employees feeling ill-equipped for the changes.
- Solution: Leaders invest in comprehensive training programs, ensuring that individuals

have the skills required for the new environment.

Overcoming resistance to change is a delicate dance that requires a deep understanding of the psychological factors at play, effective change management strategies, and a commitment to cultivating a change-ready culture. Successful leaders embrace resistance as a natural part of the change process and view it not as an obstacle but as an opportunity for growth. By addressing resistance systematically and proactively, organizations can navigate the complexities of change with resilience and emerge stronger on the other side. This chapter serves as a guide for leaders seeking to not only manage resistance but to transform it into a catalyst for positive organizational evolution.

Part IV:

Personal Leadership Plan

Chapter 11: Assessing Your Leadership Skills

"Assessing Your Leadership Skills," Chapter 11 of our journey, invites leaders on a reflective exploration of their own leadership capabilities. This chapter serves as a compass for self-discovery and growth, providing valuable insights through three key sub-chapters—Conducting a Personal SWOT Analysis, Gathering Feedback from Others, and Reflection and Analysis. Leaders embarking on this chapter will gain a nuanced understanding of their strengths, weaknesses, opportunities, and threats, fostering a path toward continuous improvement and enhanced leadership effectiveness.

❖ **What Readers Will Know:**

1. ***Conducting a Personal SWOT Analysis:***
   Dive into the world of self-awareness
   through a structured examination of your
   Strengths, Weaknesses, Opportunities, and
   Threats (SWOT). Understand how personal
   strengths can be leveraged, weaknesses
   mitigated, opportunities seized, and threats
   proactively addressed.

2. ***Gathering Feedback from Others:*** Explore
   the power of external perspectives by
   actively seeking feedback from colleagues,
   peers, and team members. Learn strategies
   for receiving constructive feedback and
   leveraging it to enhance leadership skills and
   interpersonal dynamics.

3. ***Reflection and Analysis:*** Engage in
   introspective practices that encourage
   reflection on past experiences and decisions.
   Analyze leadership challenges and triumphs,

drawing lessons that contribute to ongoing personal and professional development.

❖ Why You Need to Read This Chapter:

1. ***Self-Discovery and Growth:*** Embark on a journey of self-discovery, uncovering facets of your leadership style that may have gone unnoticed. This chapter provides tools and frameworks for personal growth, fostering a continuous evolution as a leader.

2. ***Enhanced Leadership Effectiveness:*** By understanding your strengths and addressing areas for improvement, you can enhance your leadership effectiveness. The insights gained from the assessments empower you to make informed decisions that positively impact your team and organization.

3. ***Building Resilience:*** Assessing your leadership skills equips you with the resilience needed to navigate challenges. Understanding potential threats and weaknesses allows you to proactively build strategies for overcoming obstacles.

❖ **Subchapter Overview:**

1. **Conducting a Personal SWOT Analysis: Uncover**

- Your Strengths: Identify and celebrate your unique strengths as a leader, exploring how these contribute to your effectiveness.

- Addressing Weaknesses: Confront areas where growth is needed, devising actionable plans for improvement.

- Seizing Opportunities: Recognize and capitalize on opportunities for professional and personal development.

- Mitigating Threats: Proactively assess potential threats to your leadership effectiveness, strategizing to minimize their impact.

2. Gathering Feedback from Others:

- The Importance of External Perspectives: Understand the significance of seeking feedback from colleagues, team members, and peers.

- Strategies for Effective Feedback: Learn techniques for soliciting constructive feedback and creating an environment that encourages honest input.

- Leveraging Feedback for Growth: Explore ways to translate feedback into actionable steps for personal and professional development.

3. Reflection and Analysis:

- Introspective Practices: Engage in reflective practices that deepen self-awareness and promote continuous learning.

- Analyzing Leadership Experiences: Reflect on past leadership experiences, drawing lessons that contribute to ongoing growth.

- Incorporating Insights: Integrate the insights gained from self-reflection and analysis into your leadership approach.

❖ **Who Will Benefit:**

- *Leaders at All Levels:* Whether you're an emerging leader or an experienced executive, this chapter provides valuable tools for personal and professional growth.

- *Team Leads and Managers:* Those responsible for leading teams will gain insights into enhancing their leadership effectiveness and fostering positive team dynamics.

- ***Individuals Aspiring to Leadership Roles:*** Those aspiring to leadership roles will find practical guidance for self-assessment and skill development.

- ***Organizational Development Practitioners:*** Professionals focused on organizational development will discover strategies for fostering a culture of continuous improvement.

"Assessing Your Leadership Skills" isn't just a chapter; it's a transformative guide for leaders committed to self-improvement. In a world where effective leadership is synonymous with adaptability and growth, this chapter offers the tools and insights needed to navigate the complex terrain of leadership. By actively engaging in personal SWOT analysis, seeking feedback from others, and engaging in reflective practices, leaders can pave the way for enhanced effectiveness, resilience, and sustained success. Whether you're looking to fine-tune your leadership style or embark on a profound journey of self-discovery, this chapter offers the roadmap you need to assess and elevate your leadership skills.

Conducting a Personal SWOT Analysis

"Conducting a Personal SWOT Analysis" serves as a cornerstone in the journey of self-discovery and leadership growth. A SWOT analysis—examining one's Strengths, Weaknesses, Opportunities, and Threats—provides a structured framework for individuals to gain profound insights into their leadership capabilities. This chapter delves into the intricacies of each component, offering a comprehensive guide on how leaders can leverage this tool for personal and professional development.

A Personal SWOT Analysis is a self-assessment tool that systematically examines internal Strengths and Weaknesses and external Opportunities and Threats. It provides individuals, particularly leaders, with a holistic view of their current state, enabling them to make informed decisions, capitalize on strengths, address weaknesses, seize opportunities, and navigate potential threats.

❖ Steps in Conducting a Personal SWOT Analysis:

1. Identifying Strengths:

Strengths are inherent capabilities, skills, and qualities that set individuals apart and contribute to their effectiveness.

Steps:

- *Reflect on Key Achievements*: Identify past achievements and successes that highlight your capabilities.
- *Recognize Unique Skills*: Identify skills or talents that make you stand out in your professional and personal life.

- *Seek Feedback*: Solicit feedback from colleagues, peers, and mentors to gain an external perspective on your strengths.

2. Addressing Weaknesses:

Weaknesses are areas where individuals may lack proficiency or encounter challenges.

Steps:

- *Reflect on Constructive Criticism:* Consider past feedback and areas where improvement has been suggested.
- *Identify Skill Gaps:* Recognize skills or knowledge areas that may need further development.
- *Assess Personal Habits:* Evaluate habits or behaviors that may hinder personal or professional growth.

3. Seizing Opportunities:

Opportunities are external factors or situations that individuals can leverage for personal and professional advancement.

Steps:

- *Stay Informed About Industry Trends:* Regularly update yourself on industry trends and emerging opportunities.
- *Network and Build Connections:* Cultivate professional relationships that may open doors to new opportunities.
- *Embrace Continuous Learning*: Pursue education and skill development to stay prepared for evolving opportunities.

4. Mitigating Threats:

Threats are external factors or challenges that may impede personal or professional growth.

Steps:

- *Anticipate Industry Challenges*: Stay informed about potential challenges or disruptions in your industry.

- *Develop Contingency Plans*: Identify strategies to address potential threats proactively.

- *Seek Mentorship:* Engage with mentors who have navigated similar challenges and can provide guidance.

❖ **How to Leverage the Personal SWOT Analysis:**

1. ***Strategic Decision-Making:*** Leaders can use the SWOT analysis to make strategic decisions aligned with their strengths and opportunities.

   Informed decision-making leads to more effective and impactful leadership.

2. ***Leadership Development:*** Identifying weaknesses becomes a roadmap for leadership development.

Leaders can invest in targeted training and mentorship to address areas for improvement.

3. ***Building a Leadership Brand:*** Leveraging strengths allows leaders to build a distinctive leadership brand.

Communicating these strengths contributes to a compelling and authentic leadership presence.

4. ***Navigating Challenges:*** Awareness of threats enables leaders to navigate challenges with foresight.

Proactive measures can be taken to minimize the impact of potential threats.

❖ **Overcoming Challenges in Conducting a Personal SWOT Analysis:**

1. **Overemphasis on Weaknesses:**

- *Challenge*: Individuals may focus excessively on weaknesses, leading to a skewed perspective.
- *Solution*: Balance the analysis by equally recognizing and leveraging strengths.

2. **Lack of Objectivity:**

- Challenge: Personal biases can influence the analysis.
- Solution: Seek external perspectives through feedback and constructive criticism to enhance objectivity.

3. **Neglecting Opportunities:**

- Challenge: Overlooking potential opportunities may limit growth.
- Solution: Actively scan the external environment and remain open to emerging possibilities.

Conducting a Personal SWOT Analysis is a transformative process that equips leaders with invaluable insights for self-improvement and strategic decision-making. By delving into strengths, addressing weaknesses, seizing opportunities, and mitigating threats, individuals can forge a path towards enhanced leadership effectiveness. This chapter empowers leaders to not only assess their current state but also to actively shape their future trajectory. Whether you're an experienced executive or an emerging leader, embracing the Personal SWOT Analysis offers a roadmap for continuous growth, resilience, and sustained success in the dynamic landscape of leadership.

Gathering Feedback from Others

"Gathering Feedback from Others" stands as a pivotal chapter in the journey of leadership growth and development. Acknowledging the power of external perspectives, this chapter delves into the art of seeking and utilizing feedback from colleagues, peers, and team members. Understanding the nuances of feedback collection, its role in personal and professional improvement, and strategies for creating an environment conducive to open communication are essential aspects explored in this comprehensive guide.

Gathering feedback from others involves the intentional and systematic collection of input, insights, and perspectives from individuals within and outside one's professional sphere. It is a proactive approach to understanding how one's actions, decisions, and behaviors impact those around them, providing a valuable external lens for self-reflection and growth.

❖ **Steps in Gathering Feedback from Others:**

1. **Creating a Feedback-Friendly Environment:**

A feedback-friendly environment is one that fosters open communication, trust, and a culture where feedback is viewed as constructive rather than punitive.

Steps:

- *Communicate Openness:* Leaders set the tone by expressing a genuine openness to receiving feedback.
- *Build Trust:* Cultivating trust among team members encourages honest and transparent communication.

- *Normalize Feedback:* Framing feedback as a natural and essential part of growth reduces apprehension.

2. Choosing the Right Feedback Sources:

Selecting appropriate sources for feedback ensures relevance and accuracy.

Steps:

- *Diverse Perspectives*: Seek feedback from individuals with diverse roles, experiences, and perspectives.
- *Trusted Advisors*: Identify trusted advisors or mentors who can provide candid and insightful feedback.
- *Team Input:* Gather feedback from team members who directly interact with your leadership.

3. Constructing Specific Feedback Requests:

Specific and targeted feedback requests yield actionable insights.

Steps:

- *Identify Focus Areas:* Clearly articulate the areas for which feedback is sought.
- *Use Specific Questions*: Frame questions that elicit detailed and specific responses.
- *Align with Goals*: Ensure that feedback aligns with personal and professional goals.

4. Utilizing Both Formal and Informal Channels:

Feedback can be collected through formal mechanisms like surveys or informally through one-on-one conversations.

Steps:

- *Formal Surveys:* Implement periodic surveys to gather structured feedback.

- *Informal Check-ins:* Regular informal conversations provide continuous, real-time insights.

5. Active Listening and Reflection:

Active listening involves attentively receiving feedback without immediate judgment, followed by thoughtful reflection.

Steps:

- *Listen Without Interruption*: Allow the feedback provider to share their thoughts without interruption.

- *Ask Clarifying Questions*: Seek clarification to ensure a deep understanding of the feedback.

- *Reflect on Insights*: Take time to reflect on the feedback, considering its implications for personal and professional growth.

❖ **How to Leverage Feedback Effectively:**

1. ***Identifying Patterns and Trends****:* By aggregating feedback over time, leaders can identify recurring patterns and trends.
   Consistent themes provide valuable insights into areas for improvement or strengths to leverage.

2. ***Setting Actionable Goals***: Feedback serves as a foundation for setting actionable and targeted goals.
   Leaders can align their development goals with the insights garnered from feedback.

3. ***Prioritizing Development Areas:*** Leaders prioritize development areas based on the significance and impact identified in the feedback.
   Strategic focus ensures efficient use of resources for growth.

4. ***Strengthening Interpersonal Relationships:*** Proactively seeking and utilizing feedback strengthens interpersonal relationships.

It fosters a culture of open communication and mutual respect within teams.

❖ Overcoming Challenges in Gathering Feedback:

1. Fear of Repercussions:

- *Challenge:* Individuals may fear negative consequences for providing honest feedback.
- *Solution:* Leaders assure anonymity when necessary and emphasize the constructive nature of feedback.

2. Biases in Feedback:

- *Challenge:* Feedback providers may be influenced by personal biases.

- *Solution:* Leaders actively seek feedback from a diverse range of sources to balance biases.

3. Ineffective Communication:

- *Challenge:* Poorly communicated feedback requests may yield unclear or unhelpful responses.

- *Solution*: Leaders articulate specific feedback needs and create accessible channels for communication.

Gathering feedback from others is a dynamic and iterative process that fuels continuous growth and development. Leaders who actively seek and utilize feedback demonstrate a commitment to self-improvement and the enhancement of their leadership effectiveness. This chapter serves as a guide for leaders navigating the intricacies of feedback collection, offering practical strategies for creating a feedback-friendly environment, selecting appropriate sources, and leveraging insights for meaningful growth. As leaders embrace feedback as a catalyst for positive change, they cultivate a culture of openness, trust, and collaboration within their teams and organizations.

Reflection and Analysis

"Reflection and Analysis" stands as a profound chapter in the exploration of leadership development. Rooted in the practice of introspection and thoughtful examination, this chapter delves into the importance of self-reflection for leaders. By navigating the complexities of personal experiences, decisions, and challenges, leaders can gain profound insights that contribute to ongoing growth, adaptability, and enhanced leadership effectiveness.

Reflection and analysis, in the context of leadership development, refer to the intentional and systematic process of looking inward to understand and make sense of one's experiences, decisions, and actions. It involves a deep dive into the motivations, outcomes, and lessons learned from past experiences, with the aim of extracting meaningful insights for personal and professional development.

❖ Steps in Reflection and Analysis:

1. Setting Aside Dedicated Time:

Reflective practices require intentional allocation of time for introspection.

Steps:

- *Create a Reflective Routine*: Establish regular time slots for reflection, whether daily, weekly, or monthly.
- *Eliminate Distractions*: Choose a quiet and focused environment conducive to introspection.
- *Use Tools for Guidance*: Utilize journals, prompts, or frameworks to guide the reflection process.

2. Reviewing Significant Experiences:

Leaders analyze experiences that had a significant impact on their personal or professional journey.

Steps:

- *Identify Key Moments*: Recognize experiences that stand out in memory.
- *Consider Emotional Responses*: Reflect on the emotions associated with each experience.
- *Explore Impact*: Analyze how each experience influenced decision-making and growth.

3. Identifying Patterns and Themes:

Leaders discern recurring patterns or themes across various experiences.

Steps:

- *Look for Consistencies*: Identify commonalities in reactions, decisions, or challenges.

- *Explore Motivations*: Analyze the underlying motivations driving actions.

- *Evaluate Outcomes*: Consider the results or consequences associated with similar patterns.

4. Assessing Decision-Making Processes:

Leaders scrutinize their decision-making processes to understand the factors that contribute to effective or ineffective choices.

Steps:

- *Contextualize Decisions*: Consider the context and circumstances surrounding each decision.

- *Evaluate Decision Outcomes*: Assess the outcomes and consequences of decisions.

- *Identify Decision-Making Influences*: Recognize internal and external factors that influenced choices.

5. Connecting Reflection to Goals:

Reflection gains purpose by aligning insights with personal and professional goals.

Steps:

- *Clarify Goals:* Revisit and refine personal and professional goals.
- *Map Insights to Goals:* Connect insights from reflection to specific goals.
- *Adjust Strategies:* Modify strategies and approaches based on reflections to better align with goals.

❖ How to Leverage Reflection and Analysis Effectively:

1. ***Continuous Learning and Adaptation****:*
   Leaders leverage reflection to foster a
   mindset of continuous learning.
   Insights gained inform adaptive strategies,
   ensuring relevance in dynamic environments.

2. ***Enhanced Decision-Making Skills****:* Regular
   reflection contributes to the refinement of
   decision-making skills.
   Leaders learn from past choices, evolving
   their approach to achieve better outcomes.

3. ***Cultivating Emotional Intelligence:***
   Reflection deepens emotional intelligence by
   enhancing self-awareness.
   Leaders gain a nuanced understanding of
   their emotional responses and their impact on
   others.

4. ***Strengthening Resilience:*** Examining past
   challenges and setbacks builds resilience.

Leaders learn to bounce back from adversity with a strengthened resolve.

❖ Overcoming Challenges in Reflection and Analysis:

1. Overemphasis on Negative Experiences:

- *Challenge*: Leaders may focus excessively on negative experiences, leading to a skewed perspective.
- *Solution*: Strive for balance by acknowledging both positive and negative aspects of experiences.

2. Lack of Objectivity:

- *Challenge*: Personal biases may influence the interpretation of experiences.
- *Solution:* Seek external perspectives or engage in peer discussions for a more objective view.

3. Failure to Apply Insights:

- *Challenge:* Insights gained from reflection may not be effectively translated into actionable changes.

- *Solution:* Actively connect reflections to tangible goals and strategies for practical implementation.

Reflection and analysis constitute a transformative journey for leaders committed to ongoing self-improvement and growth. By engaging in intentional introspection, leaders gain a deeper understanding of their experiences, decisions, and motivations. The insights derived from reflection contribute to enhanced decision-making skills, emotional intelligence, and resilience. This chapter serves as a guide for leaders navigating the reflective process, offering practical steps and strategies for leveraging introspection as a powerful tool for leadership development. As leaders embrace reflection as a cornerstone of their leadership journey, they not only foster personal growth but also contribute to the positive evolution of their teams and organizations.

Chapter 12: Setting Leadership Goals

"Setting Leadership Goals," Chapter 12 of our leadership exploration, is a compass guiding leader through the intricate process of goal setting for personal and professional growth. This chapter recognizes the pivotal role that well-defined goals play in shaping effective leadership. By delving into both short-term and long-term aspirations, as well as the principles of SMART goal setting, leaders gain a strategic framework for achieving success, fostering continuous improvement, and steering their teams toward excellence.

❖ **What Readers Will Know:**

1. *Importance of Goal Setting in Leadership*: Understand the significance of setting clear

and actionable goals for leadership effectiveness. Explore how goals serve as a roadmap for personal and professional development.

2. ***Short-Term and Long-Term Goal Distinctions***: Differentiate between short-term and long-term goals in the context of leadership. Recognize the unique attributes and purposes of each timeframe.

3. ***SMART Goal Setting Principles***: Embrace the SMART criteria (Specific, Measurable, Achievable, Relevant, Time-bound) for setting effective goals. Learn how SMART goals enhance clarity, accountability, and success in leadership pursuits.

❖ **Why You Need to Read This Chapter:**

1. ***Strategic Leadership Development***: Discover how goal setting serves as a strategic tool for continuous leadership

development. Learn to align personal and professional aspirations with actionable and measurable objectives.

2. ***Motivating and Inspiring Teams:*** Explore how leaders, armed with well-defined goals, can motivate and inspire their teams. Understand the ripple effect of leadership goals on team morale and performance.

3. ***Navigating Short-Term Wins and Long-Term Vision:*** Gain insights into the balance between achieving short-term wins and maintaining focus on long-term vision. Understand how a harmonious integration of both timeframes contributes to sustained success.

❖ **Subchapter Overview:**

1. Short-Term and Long-Term Goals:

Short-Term Goals:

- *Definition*: Goals achievable in the near future, typically within weeks or months.

- *Purpose*: Immediate impact, quick wins, and building momentum.

- *Strategies*: Rapid decision-making, focused efforts, and quick adaptations.

Long-Term Goals:

- *Definition*: Goals extending beyond a year, often aligned with broader career or organizational objectives.

- *Purpose*: Strategic planning, sustained growth, and profound impact.

- *Strategies*: Comprehensive planning, iterative progress tracking, and resilience in the face of challenges.

2. SMART Goal Setting in Leadership:

Specific:

- *Definition*: Clearly defined and unambiguous goals that leave no room for interpretation.
- *Example:* "Increase team productivity by implementing a new project management system."

Measurable:

- *Definition*: Goals that can be quantified to track progress and determine success.
- *Example*: "Achieve a 15% improvement in customer satisfaction scores within six months."

Achievable:

- *Definition*: Realistic goals that consider available resources and constraints.
- *Example:* "Increase quarterly sales by 10% through targeted marketing initiatives."

Relevant:

- *Definition*: Goals aligned with broader objectives, contributing to overall success.
- *Example*: "Develop a leadership training program to align with the company's talent development strategy."

Time-bound:

- *Definition*: Goals with a specific timeframe, providing a sense of urgency and accountability.
- *Example:* "Launch the new product line within the next three months to capitalize on market trends."

❖ **Who Will Benefit:**

1. *Leaders at All Levels*: Whether you're an aspiring leader or a seasoned executive, this chapter offers valuable insights for strategic goal setting.

2. ***Team Leads and Managers***: Those overseeing teams will gain practical strategies for aligning individual and team goals with organizational objectives.

3. ***Individual Contributors***: Individuals seeking personal and professional growth will find guidance on setting meaningful goals aligned with their aspirations.

4. ***Organizational Development Practitioners***: Professionals involved in organizational development will discover tools for fostering a goal-oriented culture.

"Setting Leadership Goals" is not just a chapter; it's a roadmap for leaders navigating the dynamic landscape of personal and professional growth. By exploring short-term and long-term goals and embracing the SMART criteria, leaders gain a robust framework for shaping their journey and influencing the trajectory of their teams. Whether you're looking to propel your career, inspire your team, or contribute to organizational success, this chapter equips you with the tools and perspectives needed to set goals that are not only aspirational but also actionable. Join us on this journey of strategic leadership development, where goals become the catalysts for transformation and the drivers of sustained success.

Short Term and Long Term Goals

"Short-Term and Long-Term Goals" form the foundation of effective leadership, providing a strategic roadmap for personal and professional development. In this chapter, we delve into the distinct characteristics, purposes, and strategies associated with short-term and long-term goals. By understanding the nuances of each timeframe, leaders can navigate their journey with purpose, achieve quick wins, and lay the groundwork for sustained success.

- ***Short-Term Goals:*** Short-term goals are specific, achievable objectives that can be realized in the near future, typically within weeks, months, or up to a year. These goals are instrumental in generating quick wins, building momentum, and fostering a sense of accomplishment.

- ***Long-Term Goals:*** Long-term goals extend beyond a year and are often aligned with broader career or organizational objectives. These goals require strategic planning, sustained efforts, and resilience in the face of challenges. Long-term goals provide a vision for the future and contribute to significant, lasting impact.

❖ **Short-Term Goals: Strategies for Success**

1. ***Define Clear Objectives***: Short-term goals should have specific and clearly defined objectives.

   Example: "Increase team productivity by 10% within the next three months."

2. ***Prioritize and Focus:*** Select a few key priorities to maintain focus and avoid spreading resources too thin.

Example: Prioritize initiatives that directly contribute to immediate business needs.

3. ***Rapid Decision-Making:*** In the short term, decisions need to be made swiftly to capitalize on opportunities.

   Example: Streamline decision-making processes to expedite project implementation.

4. ***Flexibility and Adaptation***: Short-term goals often require adaptability to respond to changing circumstances.

   Example: Be open to adjusting strategies based on real-time feedback and market dynamics.

5. ***Celebrate Quick Wins:*** Acknowledge and celebrate achievements to boost morale and motivation.

Example: Recognize and reward the team for meeting or exceeding short-term targets.

❖ Long-Term Goals: Strategies for Success

1. *Visionary Planning*: Long-term goals require visionary planning that aligns with overarching objectives.

   Example: Develop a five-year plan outlining milestones and key initiatives.

2. *Iterative Progress Tracking*: Track progress iteratively, regularly assessing achievements and adjusting strategies.

   Example: Implement quarterly reviews to evaluate progress toward long-term objectives.

3. *Comprehensive Resource Allocation*: Allocate resources comprehensively, considering the sustained nature of long-term goals.

Example: Invest in training programs and infrastructure to support long-term organizational growth.

4. ***Resilience in Challenges***: Long-term goals may face challenges; resilience is crucial to overcome obstacles.

   Example: Develop contingency plans and maintain a focus on the ultimate vision during setbacks.

5. ***Strategic Partnerships***: Collaborate with strategic partners to enhance capabilities and achieve long-term objectives.

   Example: Form alliances with organizations that share similar long-term goals.

❖ **Integrating Short-Term and Long-Term Goals:**

1. ***Balancing Immediate Wins and Future Vision:*** Achieving short-term wins

contributes to momentum while staying aligned with long-term vision.

Example: Implement initiatives that yield quick results while supporting the overarching strategic plan.

2. ***Communication and Alignment:*** Communicate the connection between short-term actions and long-term vision to foster alignment.

   Example: Clearly articulate how short-term projects contribute to the realization of broader goals.

3. ***Feedback and Iteration:*** Regularly seek feedback and iterate strategies to ensure alignment with evolving goals.

   Example: Conduct regular team meetings to gather input on progress and make adjustments as needed.

❖ **Overcoming Challenges:**

1. ***Balancing Urgency and Patience:***

- *Challenge*: Finding the right balance between the urgency of short-term goals and the patience required for long-term success.

- *Solution*: Develop a strategic timeline that integrates immediate priorities with a long-term vision.

2. ***Managing Resource Constraints:***

- *Challenge:* Resource constraints may pose challenges in pursuing both short-term and long-term goals simultaneously.

- *Solution*: Prioritize resource allocation based on the criticality of goals and explore creative solutions to overcome constraints.

3. ***Maintaining Team Morale:***

- *Challenge:* A focus on short-term goals may lead to burnout, while the distant nature of long-term goals may dampen morale.

- *Solution:* Foster a culture of celebration for short-term achievements and provide regular updates on progress toward long-term objectives.

"Short-Term and Long-Term Goals" represent the dual engines that drive effective leadership. Leaders who master the art of setting and integrating both short-term and long-term goals create a dynamic framework for success. By employing strategies that cater to the distinct demands of each timeframe, leaders pave the way for quick wins, sustained growth, and a transformative journey that aligns with their overarching vision. This chapter serves as a guide for leaders navigating the intricacies of goal setting, offering practical insights to achieve the delicate balance required for leadership excellence.

SMART Goal Setting in Leadership

"SMART Goal Setting in Leadership" is a cornerstone of effective leadership development, providing a structured framework for defining and pursuing objectives. In this chapter, we delve into the SMART criteria—Specific, Measurable, Achievable, Relevant, and Time-bound—offering leaders a comprehensive guide to setting goals that are not only aspirational but also actionable. By understanding the nuances of each SMART element, leaders can cultivate a culture of goal-oriented success, ensuring that their strategic vision translates into tangible and measurable outcomes.

- **SMART Goals:** SMART is an acronym that represents a set of criteria used to guide goal setting. Each letter corresponds to a different criterion, emphasizing the importance of clarity, measurability, feasibility, relevance, and a defined timeline in goal development.

❖ The SMART Criteria Explained:

1. *Specific:*

- *Definition*: Goals should be clear, precise, and unambiguous, leaving no room for misinterpretation.

- *Example*: Instead of a vague goal like "Improve team performance," a specific goal would be "Increase team productivity by 15% in the next quarter."

2. *Measurable:*

- *Definition*: Goals should be quantifiable, allowing for the tracking of progress and assessment of success.

- *Example*: Rather than stating "Enhance customer satisfaction," a measurable goal would be "Achieve a 20% improvement in customer satisfaction scores within six months."

3. *Achievable:*

- *Definition*: Goals should be realistic and attainable, considering available resources and constraints.

- *Example:* Instead of setting an unattainable goal like "Double sales in a month," an achievable goal might be "Increase quarterly sales by 10% through targeted marketing initiatives."

4. *Relevant:*

- *Definition*: Goals should align with broader objectives and be relevant to the overall mission and vision.

- *Example:* Rather than pursuing unrelated goals, a relevant goal would be "Develop a leadership training program to align with the company's talent development strategy."

5. *Time-bound:*

- *Definition:* Goals should have a specific timeframe, providing a sense of urgency and accountability.

- *Example:* Instead of leaving the timeline open-ended, a time-bound goal would be "Launch the new product line within the next three months to capitalize on market trends."

❖ Steps in Implementing SMART Goal Setting in Leadership:

1. *Clarify Objectives:* Begin by clearly defining the objectives that you aim to achieve through goal setting.

   Example: Clearly articulate whether the goal pertains to team performance, individual growth, or organizational success.

2. ***Engage Stakeholders:*** Involve relevant stakeholders in the goal-setting process to ensure alignment with broader strategies.

   Example: Seek input from team members, department heads, or external advisors to gather diverse perspectives.

3. ***Break Down Goals:*** Divide larger goals into smaller, manageable tasks to enhance clarity and facilitate progress tracking.

   Example: Instead of a broad goal like "Improve company culture," break it down into specific initiatives like "Implement weekly team-building activities."

4. ***Apply SMART Criteria:*** Evaluate each goal against the SMART criteria to ensure specificity, measurability, achievability, relevance, and a defined timeframe.

Example: Revise goals to meet SMART criteria, refining language and setting clear parameters.

5. **Create Action Plans:** Develop detailed action plans that outline the steps and resources needed to achieve each SMART goal.

Example: Identify specific action items, allocate responsibilities, and establish timelines for task completion.

6. **Regular Monitoring and Evaluation:** Continuously monitor progress toward SMART goals and evaluate outcomes to inform adjustments and improvements.

Example: Conduct regular check-ins, analyze key performance indicators, and solicit feedback to gauge progress.

❖ **Leveraging SMART Goal Setting for Leadership Success:**

1. ***Strategic Decision-Making***: SMART goals guide leaders in making strategic decisions aligned with organizational priorities.

   Example: When faced with choices, leaders can evaluate options based on their contribution to specific, measurable, and relevant goals.

2. ***Accountability and Performance Management:*** SMART goals foster accountability by providing clear expectations and criteria for performance assessment.

   Example: Teams and individuals can be held accountable for specific outcomes, making it easier to evaluate their contributions.

3. ***Enhanced Communication***: SMART goals facilitate effective communication by clearly articulating objectives and expectations.

    Example: Leaders can communicate goals with precision, ensuring that team members understand the desired outcomes and their roles in achieving them.

4. ***Continuous Improvement:*** Regularly applying the SMART criteria supports a culture of continuous improvement and adaptability.

    Example: Leaders can analyze outcomes, identify areas for improvement, and adjust strategies to align with changing circumstances.

❖ **Overcoming Challenges in SMART Goal Setting:**

1. Overemphasis on Specifics:

- *Challenge*: Overemphasizing specificity may lead to rigidity and hinder adaptability.
- *Solution*: Balance specificity with a willingness to adjust goals based on evolving circumstances.

2. Lack of Flexibility:

- *Challenge*: Rigidity in adhering to the original plan may result in missed opportunities.
- *Solution*: Encourage a flexible mindset, allowing for adjustments while maintaining the overall integrity of the goal.

3. Inadequate Resource Allocation:

- *Challenge*: Setting ambitious goals without sufficient resources may lead to frustration.

- *Solution*: Ensure realistic resource allocation to support the achievement of SMART goals.

"SMART Goal Setting in Leadership" is more than a methodology; it's a transformative approach to turning aspirations into achievements. By embracing specificity, measurability, achievability, relevance, and a defined timeline, leaders create a roadmap for success that is clear, actionable, and adaptable. This chapter serves as a guide for leaders at all levels, offering practical steps and real-world examples to illustrate the application of SMART criteria. As leaders integrate SMART goal setting into their leadership philosophy, they not only cultivate a culture of accountability and excellence but also pave the way for continuous improvement and sustained success.

Chapter 13: Strategies for Improving Leadership Skills

"Strategies for Improving Leadership Skills," Chapter 13, serves as a compass for leaders on their journey of continuous growth and development. This chapter explores targeted approaches to enhance leadership capabilities, focusing on building on strengths, addressing weaknesses, and embracing a culture of continuous evaluation and adaptation. Leaders at all levels will find practical insights and actionable strategies to elevate their effectiveness, foster personal and team excellence, and navigate the evolving landscape of leadership.

❖ **What Readers Will Know:**

1. *Building on Strengths:* Discover the power of leveraging and amplifying existing

strengths for enhanced leadership impact. Understand how a strengths-based approach contributes to increased confidence, motivation, and team engagement.

2. ***Addressing Weaknesses:*** Explore effective strategies for identifying, acknowledging, and addressing leadership weaknesses. Learn how a proactive approach to weakness management can lead to personal and professional growth.

3. ***Continuous Evaluation and Adaptation:*** Embrace the importance of ongoing self-assessment and adaptation in the dynamic realm of leadership. Understand how a commitment to continuous evaluation contributes to agility, resilience, and sustained leadership success.

❖ **Why You Need to Read This Chapter:**

1. ***Personalized Growth Strategies***: Tailor your leadership development journey by learning how to build on your unique strengths and address individual weaknesses. Acquire strategies that align with your specific leadership style and aspirations.

2. ***Team Empowerment:*** Gain insights into fostering a strengths-based culture within your team, empowering individuals to excel in areas where they shine. Understand how addressing weaknesses collectively contributes to a more resilient and adaptable team.

3. ***Adaptability in Leadership***: Navigate the fast-paced and unpredictable nature of leadership by embracing continuous evaluation and adaptation. Learn how to proactively respond to challenges and capitalize on opportunities for innovation and growth.

1. **Building on Strengths:**

- ***Maximizing Individual and Team Potential:*** Explore strategies to identify and harness individual and collective strengths within your team. Understand how aligning tasks with strengths leads to improved performance, satisfaction, and collaboration.

- ***Cultivating a Strengths-Based Culture:*** Learn to create a work environment that values and encourages the development of strengths. Understand the role of leadership in fostering a culture that celebrates individual and team accomplishments.

2. **Addressing Weaknesses:**

- ***Proactive Weakness Identification:*** Gain insights into effective methods for identifying and acknowledging personal and team weaknesses. Explore the importance of self-awareness and feedback in the weakness identification process.

- ***Strategies for Weakness Management:*** Discover practical strategies for addressing and managing weaknesses. Understand how a growth mindset and targeted skill development contribute to overcoming challenges.

3. Continuous Evaluation and Adaptation:

- ***The Importance of Regular Self-Assessment***: Explore the benefits of regular self-assessment in leadership development. Learn how self-reflection contributes to enhanced decision-making, emotional intelligence, and overall leadership effectiveness.

- ***Adapting to Evolving Leadership Dynamics***: Understand the necessity of adaptability in navigating changing leadership dynamics. Gain insights into strategies for staying agile, innovative, and resilient in the face of uncertainty.

❖ **Who Will Benefit:**

- ***Leaders at All Levels***: Whether you're a seasoned executive or an emerging leader, this chapter provides actionable strategies for continuous improvement.

- ***Team Managers and Supervisors***: Those overseeing teams will gain valuable insights into building a strengths-based team culture and addressing weaknesses proactively.

- ***Individual Contributors***: Individuals seeking to enhance their leadership skills will find practical guidance for personal growth and development.

- ***Organizational Development Practitioners***: Professionals involved in organizational development will discover tools for fostering a culture of continuous improvement and adaptation.

"Strategies for Improving Leadership Skills" is not just a chapter—it's a roadmap for leaders committed to a journey of continuous growth and excellence. By delving into the nuances of building on strengths, addressing weaknesses, and embracing continuous evaluation and adaptation, leaders can navigate the complexities of leadership with purpose and resilience. Whether you're looking to enhance your individual leadership skills or cultivate a high-performance team, this chapter equips you with the strategies and perspectives needed to thrive in the ever-evolving landscape of leadership. Join us in this exploration of personalized growth, team empowerment, and

adaptability, where leadership becomes a dynamic
and fulfilling pursuit.

Building on Strengths

"Building on Strengths" is a transformative approach to leadership development that recognizes the power of leveraging and amplifying individual and collective strengths. In this chapter, we explore the concept of strengths-based leadership, providing leaders with actionable strategies to identify, cultivate, and maximize the unique strengths within themselves and their teams. By adopting a strengths-focused mindset, leaders can create a work environment that fosters excellence, collaboration, and overall organizational success.

❖ **Strengths-Based Leadership:** Strengths-based leadership is a philosophy that emphasizes identifying and developing individual and team strengths rather than focusing on weaknesses. It involves recognizing and harnessing the unique capabilities and talents of individuals to enhance overall performance and engagement.

❖ **Steps in Building on Strengths:**

1. *Identification of Strengths:*

   • *Individual Assessment:* Encourage team members to undergo assessments such as Gallup StrengthsFinder or other strengths-based tools.

   Facilitate discussions to help individuals identify and understand their innate strengths.

   • *Observation and Feedback*: Foster a culture of open communication where team members can provide feedback on each other's strengths.

Encourage leaders to observe and recognize strengths in action, acknowledging individual contributions.

2. Alignment with Tasks and Roles:

- **Task Allocation**: Match tasks and responsibilities with the strengths of individuals within the team.

  Ensure that individuals are assigned roles where their strengths can be most effectively utilized.

- **Role Tailoring:** Modify job roles or responsibilities to better align with the strengths of team members.

  Create a flexible structure that allows for the evolution of roles based on changing strengths.

3. Cultivating a Strengths-Based Culture:

- ***Leadership Example***: Lead by example by openly discussing and leveraging your own strengths.

  Demonstrate how recognizing and utilizing strengths contributes to personal and team success.

- ***Team Recognition***: Implement a system for regularly recognizing and celebrating individual and team strengths.

  Create a platform for sharing success stories that highlight the positive impact of leveraging strengths.

4. *Professional Development and Skill Enhancement:*

- ***Focused Training***: Offer training and development opportunities that align with individual and team strengths.

Invest in programs that enhance and build upon existing strengths.

- ***Skill Synergy***: Identify areas where individual strengths can complement each other to create a synergistic team dynamic.

  Encourage collaboration and knowledge sharing to maximize the collective strength of the team.

5. *Feedback and Growth Conversations:*

- ***Regular Check-Ins:*** Conduct regular one-on-one check-ins to discuss individual strengths, progress, and areas for growth.

  Provide constructive feedback and guidance on leveraging strengths in challenging situations.

- ***Strengths-Based Performance Reviews***: Integrate strengths-based discussions into formal performance reviews.

  Use feedback sessions as an opportunity to set goals that align with individual and team strengths.

❖ **Benefits of Building on Strengths:**

1. ***Increased Engagement and Motivation:*** Employees and leaders are more engaged and motivated when they have the opportunity to leverage their strengths regularly.

   Recognizing and utilizing strengths contributes to a sense of purpose and fulfillment in work.

2. ***Enhanced Collaboration and Team Dynamics:*** Building on individual strengths

fosters a collaborative team environment where members complement each other. Synergies created by combining diverse strengths lead to innovative problem-solving and improved team performance.

3. ***Improved Performance and Productivity:*** Aligning tasks with individual strengths results in improved performance and increased productivity.

Individuals are more likely to excel in areas where they naturally excel, leading to higher-quality outputs.

4. ***Positive Organizational Culture:*** A strengths-based culture contributes to a positive organizational environment where employees feel valued and empowered.

Recognition and celebration of strengths create a sense of belonging and loyalty.

5. ***Adaptability and Resilience:*** Leveraging strengths enhances adaptability and resilience in the face of challenges. Individuals and teams are better equipped to navigate change when they can draw on their inherent capabilities.

❖ Overcoming Challenges:

1. *Avoiding Stereotypes:*

- *Challenge*: Stereotypes about certain strengths may limit the recognition of diverse talents.
- *Solution*: Encourage an open-minded approach and avoid pigeonholing individuals based on preconceived notions.

2. *Balancing Weaknesses:*

- *Challenge*: Exclusively focusing on strengths may neglect areas that require improvement.
- *Solution:* Acknowledge and address weaknesses where necessary, ensuring a

balanced approach to personal and team development.

3. Continuous Feedback Loop:

- *Challenge:* Building on strengths requires a continuous feedback loop, which may be challenging in fast-paced environments.

- *Solution:* Establish regular feedback mechanisms and create a culture that values ongoing communication.

"Building on Strengths" is not just a leadership strategy; it's a philosophy that transforms how individuals and teams approach their work. By identifying and amplifying strengths, leaders create an environment where excellence is not just encouraged but becomes a natural outcome. This chapter serves as a guide for leaders seeking to harness the unique talents within their teams, fostering a culture of empowerment, collaboration, and sustained success. Whether you're a seasoned executive or an emerging leader, the principles of building on strengths provide a roadmap for creating a workplace where individuals thrive, teams excel, and the organization as a whole achieves new heights. Join us on this journey of recognizing, cultivating, and maximizing the strengths that define exceptional leadership.

Addressing Weaknesses

"Addressing Weaknesses" is a pivotal chapter in the journey of leadership development, acknowledging the importance of self-awareness and proactive growth. While leveraging strengths is crucial, effective leaders recognize that addressing weaknesses is equally vital for personal and professional advancement. In this chapter, we delve into the strategies, mindset shifts, and actionable steps that empower leaders to identify, acknowledge, and overcome weaknesses, fostering a culture of continuous improvement and resilience.

❖ **Addressing Weaknesses:** Addressing weaknesses involves the intentional and proactive identification, acknowledgment, and management of areas where an individual may have limitations or room for improvement. It is a process of self-reflection and targeted efforts to enhance skills, competencies, and overall effectiveness.

❖ Steps in Addressing Weaknesses:

1. Self-Reflection and Assessment:

- ***Identifying Weaknesses:*** Engage in honest self-reflection to identify areas where skills or behaviors may be considered weaknesses.

  Seek feedback from peers, mentors, or trusted advisors to gain external perspectives on potential areas for improvement.

- ***Prioritizing Weaknesses:*** Prioritize identified weaknesses based on their impact on personal and professional goals.

  Determine which weaknesses are most critical to address in the current phase of leadership development.

2. **Developing a Growth Mindset:**

- ***Embracing a Growth Mindset:*** Adopt a growth mindset that views weaknesses as opportunities for learning and development. Understand that abilities can be cultivated and improved through effort, dedication, and a willingness to learn.

- ***Resilience in the Face of Challenges:*** Cultivate resilience by reframing challenges as learning experiences.

  Embrace setbacks as stepping stones toward improvement rather than viewing them as insurmountable obstacles.

3. **Seeking Targeted Learning Opportunities:**

- ***Formal Education and Training:*** Identify relevant courses, workshops, or training programs to address specific weaknesses.

Invest time in formal education to acquire new knowledge and skills aligned with identified areas for improvement.

- ***Mentorship and Coaching:*** Seek mentorship or coaching from individuals with expertise in the identified areas of weakness.

  Leverage the guidance and insights of mentors to navigate challenges and accelerate personal growth.

4. Setting Realistic Goals for Improvement:

- ***SMART Goal Setting:*** Apply the SMART criteria (Specific, Measurable, Achievable, Relevant, Time-bound) to set clear goals for addressing weaknesses.

  Break down overarching improvement goals into smaller, manageable steps.

- ***Progress Monitoring:*** Regularly monitor progress toward improvement goals.

  Celebrate small victories and adjust strategies as needed to stay on track.

5. Feedback and Accountability:

- ***Feedback Channels:*** Establish open channels for receiving constructive feedback from colleagues, team members, and superiors.

  Create a feedback loop that facilitates continuous improvement and prevents the stagnation of weaknesses.

- ***Accountability Partnerships:*** Form accountability partnerships with peers or mentors who can provide support and encouragement.

Share progress, challenges, and strategies for addressing weaknesses with accountability partners.

❖ **Benefits of Addressing Weaknesses:**

1. ***Personal Growth and Development:*** Proactively addressing weaknesses contributes to ongoing personal growth and development.

   Individuals become more adaptable, versatile, and resilient in the face of challenges.

2. ***Enhanced Leadership Effectiveness***: Leaders who address their weaknesses become more effective in guiding and inspiring their teams.

   Improved leadership skills positively impact team dynamics and overall organizational success.

3. ***Increased Self-Awareness:*** The process of addressing weaknesses fosters heightened self-awareness.

   Individuals gain a deeper understanding of their strengths, weaknesses, and areas for potential growth.

4. ***Cultivation of a Learning Culture:*** Leaders who openly address weaknesses contribute to a culture of continuous learning within their teams.

   Team members are inspired to embrace a growth mindset and pursue their own development opportunities.

5. ***Strategic Decision-Making:*** Leaders who address weaknesses strategically enhance their decision-making capabilities.

They become more adept at recognizing potential pitfalls, mitigating risks, and making informed choices.

❖ Overcoming Challenges:

1. *Fear of Vulnerability:*

- *Challenge*: Fear of appearing vulnerable may hinder individuals from acknowledging and addressing weaknesses.
- *Solution*: Foster a culture that values vulnerability and views it as a strength rather than a weakness.

2. *Overwhelm with Multiple Weaknesses:*

- *Challenge*: Leaders may feel overwhelmed when faced with multiple weaknesses.
- *Solution:* Prioritize weaknesses based on their impact and address them systematically, one at a time.

3. *Resistance to Change:*

- *Challenge*: Resistance to change may impede efforts to address weaknesses.
- *Solution*: Communicate the benefits of addressing weaknesses, emphasizing personal and professional growth.

"Addressing Weaknesses" is a courageous and transformative journey that distinguishes exceptional leaders. By embracing weaknesses as opportunities for growth, leaders not only enhance their own effectiveness but also inspire a culture of continuous improvement within their teams. This chapter serves as a guide, offering practical steps, mindset shifts, and real-world examples to support leaders in their quest for ongoing development. Whether you're a seasoned executive or an emerging leader, addressing weaknesses is a pathway to unlocking your full potential and becoming a resilient, adaptable, and impactful leader. Join us in this exploration of self-discovery and growth as we navigate the terrain of addressing

weaknesses with purpose and determination.

Continuous Evaluation and Adaptation

"Continuous Evaluation and Adaptation" represents the heartbeat of effective leadership—a dynamic process of self-awareness, learning, and proactive adjustment. In this chapter, we explore the transformative journey of leaders committed to ongoing improvement. By embracing a mindset of continuous evaluation and adaptation, leaders not only stay relevant in an ever-evolving landscape but also foster a culture of resilience, innovation, and sustained success.

❖ **Continuous Evaluation and Adaptation:** Continuous evaluation and adaptation refer to the systematic and ongoing process of assessing one's performance, strategies, and approaches, with a commitment to making timely adjustments. It involves a cyclical loop of reflection, analysis, and refinement to stay aligned with goals, respond to changing circumstances, and optimize leadership effectiveness.

❖ Steps in Continuous Evaluation and Adaptation:

1. **Regular Self-Assessment:**

   - ***Reflection Practices***: Cultivate regular self-reflection practices to assess personal and professional experiences.

     Allocate dedicated time for introspection to understand strengths, weaknesses, and areas for improvement.

   - ***Goal Alignment:*** Ensure personal and professional goals remain aligned with overarching objectives.

Regularly evaluate whether current pursuits contribute to long-term aspirations and organizational success.

2. Feedback and Input Gathering:

- ***Stakeholder Feedback***: Solicit feedback from peers, team members, and superiors to gain diverse perspectives.

    Create a feedback-friendly environment that encourages open communication and constructive input.

- ***Surveys and Assessments***: Utilize surveys and assessments to gather quantitative data on leadership effectiveness.

    Analyze trends and patterns to identify areas that require attention or improvement.

3. Data-Driven Decision Making:

- ***Key Performance Indicators (KPIs):*** Establish and monitor KPIs relevant to leadership goals and organizational objectives.

  Leverage data to make informed decisions and measure the impact of leadership strategies.

- ***Benchmarking:*** Engage in benchmarking activities to compare leadership practices with industry best practices.

Identify areas where adaptation is necessary to align with or surpass established benchmarks.

4. **Adaptive Leadership Strategies:**
- ***Scenarios and Contingency Planning***: Anticipate potential challenges and develop contingency plans for various scenarios.

Foster an adaptive mindset that allows for quick adjustments in response to unforeseen circumstances.

- ***Innovation and Experimentation:*** Encourage a culture of innovation and experimentation within the team.

  Embrace new approaches and ideas, and be willing to pivot when experimentation reveals more effective methods.

5. Professional Development and Learning:

- ***Continuous Learning Plan:*** Develop a continuous learning plan that includes ongoing education, skill development, and exposure to emerging trends.
  Stay informed about industry advancements and incorporate new knowledge into leadership practices.

- *Networking and Knowledge Exchange:* Engage in networking opportunities to exchange insights with other leaders.

  Participate in forums, conferences, and industry events to broaden perspectives and stay connected with evolving practices.

❖ **Benefits of Continuous Evaluation and Adaptation:**

1. *Resilience in Leadership:* Leaders who continuously evaluate and adapt build resilience in the face of challenges.

   The ability to pivot and adjust strategies enhances adaptability and minimizes the impact of setbacks.

2. *Innovation and Creativity:* A commitment to continuous evaluation fosters an environment of innovation.

Leaders are more open to creative solutions and novel approaches to problem-solving.

3. ***Optimized Performance:*** Regular evaluation and adaptation lead to optimized performance.

   Leaders can refine their approaches, eliminate inefficiencies, and enhance overall effectiveness.

4. ***Proactive Problem Solving:*** Leaders who embrace continuous evaluation are proactive in identifying and addressing issues.

   The ability to foresee challenges allows for timely interventions and strategic problem-solving.

5. ***Adaptive Leadership Culture:*** The practice of continuous evaluation extends beyond

individual leaders to shape an adaptive organizational culture.

Teams and departments become more responsive to change, fostering a culture of agility and innovation.

❖ **Overcoming Challenges:**

1. ***Complacency and Routine***:
   - *Challenge*: Leaders may become complacent in routine practices, hindering the evaluation process.
   - *Solution:* Foster a culture that encourages questioning the status quo and challenges the comfort of routine.

2. ***Resistance to Change:***
   - *Challenge:* Team members or leaders may resist change, impeding adaptation efforts.

- *Solution:* Communicate the benefits of change, emphasizing growth, improvement, and increased effectiveness.

3. *Overemphasis on Short-Term Results:*

- *Challenge*: A focus on short-term results may overshadow the importance of long-term continuous evaluation.

- *Solution*: Educate stakeholders about the long-term benefits of adaptive leadership and sustained success.

"Continuous Evaluation and Adaptation" is not a destination; it's a dynamic journey that propels leaders toward sustained excellence. In this chapter, we've explored the critical steps, mindset shifts, and benefits associated with leaders committed to ongoing improvement. Whether you're a seasoned executive or an emerging leader, the principles of continuous evaluation and adaptation offer a roadmap for navigating the complexities of leadership with agility and resilience. Join us in this exploration of self-discovery, learning, and growth as we embrace the transformative power of continuous evaluation and adaptation in the pursuit of leadership excellence.

Conclusion

As we arrive at the culmination of this comprehensive exploration into the realms of leadership, it is fitting to reflect upon the intricate tapestry of principles, strategies, and insights that constitute the essence of leadership excellence. This journey has traversed the diverse landscape of leadership—from foundational elements like communication and integrity to the nuanced complexities of team building, continuous learning, and adaptive leadership strategies.

❖ Navigating the Leadership Odyssey:

The odyssey of leadership is a dynamic and transformative expedition, one that demands introspection, resilience, and an unwavering commitment to growth. Throughout this book, we have ventured into the heart of leadership, unveiling the significance of self-awareness, the strategic deployment of strengths, and the art of addressing weaknesses with purpose.

- ***Self-Awareness as the North Star:*** At the core of effective leadership lies a profound self-awareness—a compass guiding leaders through the complexities of decision-making, communication, and relationship-building. The chapters on self-awareness and building on strengths underscore that leadership excellence commences with a deep understanding of one's own strengths and areas for development.

- ***Crafting Vision and Strategy:*** From the foundation of self-awareness, leaders ascend to the pinnacle of visionary thinking and strategic planning. Crafting a compelling vision, aligning goals, and fostering a culture of innovation become the keystones of effective leadership. As leaders, the ability to translate visions into actionable plans distinguishes the extraordinary from the ordinary.

- ***Team Dynamics and Collaboration***: The chapters on team building and collaboration delve into the intricacies of fostering a cohesive and empowered team. Leaders are architects of environments where diversity is celebrated, collaboration is nurtured, and every team member is empowered to contribute their unique strengths. Effective team leadership involves not only harnessing individual strengths but also navigating conflicts and fostering a shared sense of purpose.

- ***Continuous Learning and Adaptation***: In the ever-evolving landscape of leadership, the commitment to continuous learning and adaptation emerges as a linchpin for sustained success. Leaders who recognize the imperative of staying agile, learning from experiences, and adapting strategies are not only future-ready but also catalysts for organizational resilience.

❖ Embracing Change and Innovation:

The journey of leadership extends beyond the present, beckoning leaders to embrace the future with open arms. As we peer into the horizon, the landscape is characterized by unprecedented challenges and boundless opportunities. The principles outlined in this book serve as a compass for leaders navigating the tides of change and driving innovation within their organizations.

- ***Leadership's Role in Change***: The role of leadership in driving change is not merely a strategic imperative but a transformative journey. Leaders who champion change inspire their teams to embrace uncertainty, navigate challenges, and see change as a vehicle for growth. The chapters on overcoming resistance to change and leading innovative teams illuminate the path for leaders who seek to navigate the dynamics of change with finesse.

- ***Adapting Strategies for Tomorrow***: The final chapters on continuous evaluation and adaptation, addressing weaknesses, and building on strengths encapsulate the essence of future-ready leadership. The ability to assess, adapt, and refine strategies positions leaders as architects of resilience, capable of steering their organizations through the winds of change.

❖ **Final Reflections and Words of Encouragement:**

As we draw the final curtain on this exploration of leadership, it is essential to offer reflections and words of encouragement to the leaders who have embarked on this odyssey.

- ***Leadership as a Dynamic Journey:*** Leadership is not a static destination but a dynamic journey—one marked by triumphs, challenges, and continuous growth. Every step taken, every lesson learned, and every challenge overcome contributes to the evolution of leadership excellence.

- ***Legacy of Leadership Impact:*** Consider the legacy you are crafting through your leadership. It transcends the immediate outcomes and shapes the culture, values, and success of your organization. Leadership, at its core, is about making a lasting impact that reverberates beyond the present moment.

- ***Cultivating a Culture of Excellence***: Leaders, be torchbearers of a culture of excellence. The principles elucidated in this book extend beyond individual leadership—they form the bedrock of organizational culture. Strive to create an environment where excellence is not only encouraged but expected.

- ***Commitment to Continuous Growth***: Leadership excellence is a commitment to ongoing growth and development. The insights gleaned from this book are not conclusions but catalysts for continuous learning, skill refinement, and personal development. View every experience as an opportunity for growth, and commit to the journey of perpetual improvement.

- ***Connecting and Collaborating***: Leadership is not a solitary endeavor. Connect with fellow leaders, mentors, and industry peers. Engage in conversations that elevate the discourse on effective leadership, share insights, and collectively contribute to the growth of the leadership community. In collaboration, leadership finds strength and resilience.

In conclusion, this book has unfolded a narrative of leadership that transcends the conventional boundaries. It is a narrative that celebrates self-awareness, visionary thinking, collaboration, resilience, and the unyielding commitment to growth. As leaders, you are not merely navigating the present; you are shaping the future.

May your leadership journey be marked by purpose, impact, and the unwavering belief that the best is yet to come. Whether you are a seasoned executive or an emerging leader, the principles shared in this book serve as a compass guiding you through the complexities of leadership. As you stand at the crossroads of your leadership odyssey, may you continue to lead with authenticity, inspire with vision, and influence with unwavering integrity.

Here's to the leaders who dare to dream, inspire those around them, and leave an indelible mark on the canvas of leadership excellence. As you step forward into the future, may your leadership continue to be a beacon of inspiration and a force for positive change. The odyssey of leadership is ongoing, and with each step, you contribute to a narrative that shapes not only your story but the collective narrative of leadership excellence.